NEIGHBOURS

OTHER BOOKS BY JAMES ORAM

Hogan: The story of a son of Oz
The People's Pope
The Business of Pop
The Hellraisers (with Jim Fagan)

ABOUT THE AUTHOR

James Oram has worked in newspapers and magazines in London and Sydney. He is now a special writer and columnist for the News Ltd group of newspapers in Sydney, has covered a dozen royal tours, three papal tours, and major stories in Australia, the South Pacific and South-East Asia, including the guerilla war in the southern Philippines, the destruction of Darwin by Cyclone Tracy, the rebellion in Vanuatu, the heroin trade in Thailand, the Los Angeles Games, the America's Cup in Perth and the army coup in Fiji. Show business keeps him occupied when he is not travelling and soap operas are his relaxation.

NEIGHBOURS
BEHIND THE SCENES

JAMES ORAM

ANGUS
& ROBERTSON
PUBLISHERS

For Marie Ussher with love

ANGUS & ROBERTSON PUBLISHERS

16 Golden Square, London W1R 4BN,
United Kingdom and Unit 4, Eden Park,
31 Waterloo Road, North Ryde, NSW,
Australia 2113

First published in the United Kingdom by
Angus & Robertson (UK) in 1988

Reprinted 1988 (six times)

Copyright © James Oram 1988

Typeset in Great Britain by
New Faces, Bedford

Designed by Mark Foster

Printed in Great Britain by
Scotprint Ltd, Musselburgh, Scotland

British Library Cataloguing in Publication Data

Oram, James
Neighbours
  I. Television drama series in English. Neighbours
  I. Title
  791.45'72

ISBN 0 207 16075 9

CONTENTS

INTRODUCTION

'Neighbours' was first screened in Australia on 18 March 1985, and in Britain on 27 October 1986. The period between these dates, the months, weeks, days and episodes, are a lifetime in the soap opera world. In that time soap people can live and die, go to hospital, jail or Brisbane, commit murder, adultery or hari kari, get involved in car crashes, plane crashes and stock market crashes, be afflicted with cancer, AIDS or gout, get married and divorced, engaged and jilted, have babies, change jobs, addresses and spouses. Nothing is impossible in a soap opera; the impossible is expected. So in this look behind the scenes of 'Neighbours', the phenomenally successful Australian serial, some characters and events will be new to British readers. Other characters may have already disappeared. The front entrance of a soap opera is a swinging door through which characters come and go with remarkable frequency. The 'Neighbours' door swings as freely as any.

1

Top of the Ratings

The telephone shattered Colin Stanley-Hill's until then untroubled sleep. Forcing open his eyes, he glanced at the bedside clock and noting it was 3am called down a thousand curses upon those who felt the need to ring at such unseemly hours. He barked his name into the receiver.

'Colin,' said a well-rounded voice. 'It's the Palace here.'

He shot upright like he'd just sat on a red-back spider. 3am! The Palace! Something must be dreadfully wrong, a constitutional crisis, perhaps, an abdication ... Whatever, it was obviously an emergency.

'Yes?' he said anxiously.

Stanley-Hill was well known to Buckingham Palace. He was Australian Court Correspondent and had been on the Queen Mother's staff before settling in Australia as a film-maker and dealer in fine art. He was now living in the leafy, well-heeled Sydney suburb of Woollahra. He steeled himself for the worst.

'Yes?' he repeated, now wide awake.

'Colin, what's happening in "Neighbours?"' inquired the voice. A man not noted for reticence, Stanley-Hill was for a moment stuck for words as he mentally ticked off his neighbours, a queen's counsel up the road, a merchant banker opposite, a former premier around the corner, and wondered what they'd been up to. He said something more like a strangled cry than the Queen's English.

'"Neighbours", man, "Neighbours". We all watch it here. The Queen's very interested to know what stage the serial has reached in Australia.'

'Yes, yes, it's quite popular here too,' said Stanley-Hill, searching for the right words as it dawned on him the voice was speaking of a soap opera, not the people living around him. It further dawned on him that 'Neighbours' wasn't on his viewing schedule. 'Look,' he said, 'to be truthful, I'm afraid you're probably talking to the one person in Australia who's never watched it.'

The voice turned a trifle cold. 'You might care to see it some time. Everyone wants to know.' A bit of idle chat was exchanged and the Palace hung up.

'Neighbours' had been given the royal seal of approval. Unfortunately for the Australian producers, this did not allow them to hang up a plaque bearing the royal coat of arms and the legend: 'By Appointment to Her Majesty Queen Elizabeth the Second.' The Royal Warrant is granted only to businesses that have supplied the Royal Household for three years. 'Neighbours' hadn't been in existence for three years but it was nice to know the best people were among its viewers.

The residents of Buckingham Palace, with the suspected exception of Prince Philip, are not the only royal fans. There's at least one more in the Gloucestershire mansion, Highgrove House. The Princess of Wales takes an interest not only in 'Dallas' and 'Dynasty', but also in the comings and goings of Ramsay Street. Kylie Minogue was hoping to engage her on the very same subject when they met after the New South Wales Royal Bicentennial Concert at the Sydney Entertainment Centre in January 1988. Along with Cliff Richard, John Denver, Olivia Newton-John, Peter Allen, Pamela Stephenson and Jon Farnham, Kylie had entertained the Prince and Princess of Wales and the Australian Prime Minister, Bob Hawke. As is customary after a royal performance, the stars lined up like the changing of the guard to meet Charles and Diana, shake hands, exchange a few words and pose.

Kylie was near the end of the line and was suffering from nerves by the time the Princess got to her. Diana was introduced. Press cameras flashed. 'I was going to ask her about the show but I got too nervous and excited,' said Kylie. 'So we talked about the concert instead.'

Prince Charles showed he was not a viewer. 'And what is the series you are in?' he asked after being introduced to Kylie.

Kylie explained.

'I'll have to make a point of watching it,' he said politely.

Maybe he will. Then he can join the other 20 million or so who settle down to watch it every weekday in Britain and Australia, a phenomenal audience for a programme many adults swear they have never seen, then hope their nose doesn't grow like Pinocchio's, and which many critics have condemned.

It wasn't always that way. At first 'Neighbours' was anything but a success and was cancelled by the television network that originally commissioned the soap opera, or soap, as the genre is more popularly known. Another network, Ten, took it up, uncertain at first but confident it had the ingredients to become a ratings winner. A considerable sum of money went into promotion. And it was during such a promotion that the broadcasting network realised that not only did it have a valuable commodity but also a very considerable success on its hands.

In March 1987, the Sydney afternoon newspaper, the *Daily Mirror*, ran a contest for four readers to meet some of the cast. The meeting took place at a fun park outside Sydney called Wonderland. More than 10,000 fans turned up, crying, cheering, jostling and finally breaking through barricades in an attempt to be near, even to touch, the actors who included Guy Pearce, Elaine Smith, Annie Jones and Craig McLachlan.

Looking at the seething mass, the network's publicity chief, Brian Walsh, shook his head and called it 'crazy', at the same time realising he was witnessing the mild, relatively harmless hysteria that occasionally spreads in the presence of certain pop stars. With television personalities it happened less; they were too familiar, too much a part of everyday life, appearing in the home each weekday night, regular visitors like an aunt or the kids from next door. Like neighbours, in fact.

But here something was stirring. There was a chemistry between the cast and the public of the sort promoters dream about – the mysterious IT! Bon Jovi had IT and so did George Michael and now, it seemed, did a fairly inexpensive soap opera.

Walsh planned the next outing for the following month at the Sydney Royal Easter Show, a once-a-year mixture of agricultural exhibitions and fun fair attracting more than a million people, where country

'Neighbours' hysteria as fans struggle for a glimpse of the stars on stage at Westfield (Photo: News Ltd)

folk wear ties and coats and city slickers silly hats. Kylie and Jason Donovan were the attractions and from the moment they appeared on the Ten Network stand in the Hordern Pavilion, the crowd, mostly young people, went wild. In a great wave, they swept forward, crushing each other, trampling some underneath, screaming, sobbing,

'At one stage the police and guards had to literally pull me out' –
Jason Donovan, the object of the attention of thousands of fans
(Photo: News Ltd)

not as bad as those nightmarish scenes sometimes occurring in football stadiums when matters get out of hand, but ugly enough.

Four kids were treated on the spot by para-medics, an 11-year-old girl was taken to hospital with minor injuries after being crushed. For forty minutes fifty police and officials heaved and hauled the kids out of the way to save them from themselves and Kylie and Jason from being swamped. Said one Ten Network staff member: 'We had to pull kids out of the crowd because they were getting crushed. Some of them had been waiting two hours for Jason and Kylie to arrive.' Grabbing a microphone, Jason appealed to the audience to calm down but they weren't hearing anything except their own screams and sobs.

'It was obvious someone was going to get hurt,' he said. 'I know we were in danger ourselves but we were really more worried about the kids than us. I'd made a lot of public appearances but had never seen anything like this before.'

Neither had Kylie, who is built on the lines of a feather and would have been whisked away to heaven knows where had she been caught in the surge. She said, 'It was incredible. There were thousands of kids watching us and they were quiet. Then as soon as we started signing autographs they started crushing towards us. We tried to get them to calm down but they were too excited. They kept pushing forward and there was nothing we could do to stop them.'

The pair were eventually bundled into a police paddywagon and taken from the showground to their motel. Inspector Brett Winthrop, in charge of the operation, likened the reaction to the hysteria surrounding the Beatles' 1964 visit to Australia, an occasion imprinted in the memories of older people but one that occurred before Jason and Kylie were born.

'It was a case of too many people in too small a space,' the Inspector said. 'There were hundreds of teenage girls between ten and thirteen years old all trying to get closer to the stars. It was hysteria.'

The story made the front pages of Sydney newspapers, nice as far as publicity went, but not for officials of the Royal Easter Show. They immediately banned the cast of 'Neighbours' from their not inconsiderable precinct. This made more headlines. The Ten Network went into urgent consultation with officials and police and a day later, after a better area was found within the showground, the ban was lifted. Again the newspapers obliged with stories. 'Neighbours' was up and running with a clear field ahead.

Then came the wedding. The marriage between Scott Robinson and Charlene Mitchell, the characters played by Jason and Kylie, sent the ratings in Australia soaring the entire week given over to the ceremony and the events surrounding it.

Weddings in soaps are carried out with a maximum of drama like a dying scene in grand opera; great emphasis is placed on weddings. They are treated with a lot of respect, especially by producers.

'Neighbours' producer, Marie Trevor, understands. 'I think the only consideration we face is if we're going to have a wedding, let's do

Illusion or reality? Some people confused the fictional wedding with fact. Kylie and Jason promoting the series – and the wedding of Charlene and Scott (Photo: News Ltd)

it in a rating period, of course, because of the costs involved in holding a wedding and doing it well. But the wedding has to be true to the characters and true to the story. I don't think the writers set out to be terribly moralistic about it. We would never marry off characters for the sake of it. The audience is pretty cluey. They become involved in these characters and invite them into their homes five nights a week. I don't think we would ever consider breaking that trust.'

To promote the occasion of the wedding, Jason and Kylie appeared at a cavernous shopping complex in Paramatta, in the western, predominately working-class area of Sydney. They walked on stage; below them was a semicircle of twenty guards and ten police to ensure fans wouldn't bruise them too much, then they cut a wedding cake and attempted to give pieces to the 4,000 or so who had been waiting for a couple of hours. But the kids out there beyond the security men wanted more. In their eyes was a look of determination like soldiers about to attack. And attack they did, armed with only autograph books and a surge of adrenalin. The guards fought gallantly but were beaten back at first.

'At one stage the police and guards had to literally pull me out,' said Jason. Children parted from parents howled. Shopkeepers glanced anxiously at their plate-glass windows. Surviving the attack, the guards finally triumphed, then attended the casualties. One woman, Judith Toomey, said she was pushed to the ground near the stage and lost count of the number of people who trod on her. Several others fainted. After some order was restored Jason said, 'I'm worried these young girls can get so carried away that they actually cause risk to other people. Some of the kids had apparently been waiting two or three hours. By the time we arrived, they were so excited they were just crushing forward … It really concerned me kids act like this.'

Kylie was shaken. 'I love the fact they care about us but we want to be able to do more public appearances without this sort of risk,' she said after the pandemonium had subsided to a gentle shriek. 'I felt really shaken by the danger when the kids went mad and started pushing.'

News of the disturbance confirmed the view of the managers of the Ten Network: they had a runaway success on their hands. And it was a success that would soon be echoed in Britain.

2

Anatomy of a Soap

Television soap operas are, of course, descended from radio. The first, 'Painted Dreams', written by an Ohio schoolteacher, Irna Phillips, was broadcast by Chicago station WGN in 1930 as a device to attract female interest by focusing on the family, home-making, romance and relationships in general. Three years later the networks had picked up the idea and the soaps, named after the big soap-manufacturing companies such as Procter and Gamble which sponsored them, were a part of American entertainment, attracting vast audiences enticed into regular, habitual viewing.

Once the television networks noted the popularity of soaps they leapt on to them with enthusiasm because, above all, they were cheap to produce. The networks were prepared to spend big money on prime-time shows but they needed a filler for the long daytime hours, programmes that wouldn't cost them an arm and a leg. The action in soaps basically takes place indoors, in lounges, kitchens, bedrooms, lawyers' offices, restaurants, executive suites, hospitals, pubs and small shops. The sets can be built cheaply, two or three close by each other in the studio. Shooting in video is also much cheaper than on film. Modern sophisticated video equipment allows the soap to go outdoors if it so desires, even to exotic places, but mostly it stays close to the easily built and just as easily dismantled sets.

Costs are kept low by turning out scripts on an assembly line. (The scripts of 'Neighbours' cost only £800 an episode.) The show's head writer determines long-term story developments and provides a written summary of the action to occur in each episode. This outline is then turned over to associate writers, who fill in the dialogue to be spoken.

But the area where money is saved most is in the salary of the performers. By comparison with those in prime-time shows, the soap stars are paid a pittance. One lead actor of the American soap, 'Capitol', was getting a mere $US3,000 a week, which he considered peanuts but accepted on the grounds it was regular. 'That's why we refer to soaps as cereals – they keep everything so regular,' he said.

The cast of 'Neighbours', even though they are in a prime-time show, are not paid fortunes. For a 70-hour week they get as little as £240 and few more than £1,000. 'Dallas' and 'Dynasty' reward their stars with more money per week than the entire budget of 'Neighbours'.

'Lorry drivers get more than soap stars in Australia,' said Anne Haddy (Helen Daniels). Francis Bell (Max Ramsay) thought he wasn't being paid enough for his work and the demands of his character. His contract was not renewed. Soap contracts are written in a way that allows actors to be removed at short notice.

Even in the expensive prime-time soaps such as 'Dallas', 'Dynasty', 'Knots Landing', 'Falcon Crest', and 'The Colbys', producers frequently look for ways to rid themselves of actors who are costing too much. The problem is the more popular a show the greater the salary demands of the stars, many of whom were unknown a year or so before and now believe they are Paul Newman or Jane Fonda. 'If you lop off a lot of $50,000-an-episode actors, you save a decent amount of money,' said the pragmatic executive producer of 'Dallas', Leonard Katzman.

'Dallas' is of course the leader in the soap opera world, managing in the words of British soap producer Bill Smethurst to 'make 'em laugh, make 'em cry, but above all make 'em wait'. But over the years Australia too has pumped out a number of soaps, some reasonable, many trashy.

The first, the gloriously tacky 'Number 96' was swiftly followed by such as 'The Sullivans', 'Sons and Daughters', 'The Restless Years', 'Prisoner Cell Block H', 'The Young Doctors' and more recently 'A Country Practice', 'Home and Away', 'Richmond Hill' and, of course, 'Neighbours'.

Episode 175

'Most people in Ramsay Street are thoroughly fed up with Max getting them up at 5am with his tape of animal noises. The exceptions are Daphne and Zoe. Daphne is in love and nothing can upset her; Zoe thought it was a great giggle. Madge is not having a good day. Apart from the early start, she is attacked by a mugger and only avoids serious injury by the fortuitous arrival of Jim. And when she gets to the prison, it is to discover that she is no longer wanted and has to leave without even getting inside. The one bright spot is the kindness of Jim and she begins to see him as something more than just her brother's best friend. Paul gets a new job as a junior executive in a large company and he feels he's at last on the way to realising his ambitions. His attitude to women, however, is not so commendable. Terry has hurt him deeply and he lashes out. In his view, women are to be used and use them he's going to. However, in the process he infuriates Jim and upsets Helen and Lucy. Danny is still trying to get the money together to take Marcie to Surfers Paradise and, against his better wishes, is talked into moonlighting as a chicken by Clive. He nearly comes unstuck when he is locked out of Clive's house and has to wear his chicken suit home. He escapes from Max who ends up with a handful of feathers. The next morning Max threatens Clive about keeping his chickens to himself.'

This 'Neighbours' synopsis, chosen at random, is typical of a soap opera. Personal problems, some wrong-doing, romance and a little humour are the ingredients of soaps, no matter if they are low budget productions like 'Neighbours' or expensive numbers in the 'Dallas' and 'Dynasty' mould. There is nothing new in soaps; a multi-million dollar deal J.R. Ewing might make in 'Dallas' can be translated to 'Neighbours' as concern over the Ramsay family budget. What fascinates, and often irritates, the infrequent viewer of soaps, is the tangled threads woven into the plots, the complications of lives, the frustrated passions that seethe, the way a character cannot get up to make a cup of tea without it becoming a subplot.

One thing's for certain, without the tangled threads of romance, soaps wouldn't last a week, or twenty-four hours in some cases. In fact there wouldn't be a soap industry. 'What really works is romance and lots of it,' said Al Rabin, executive producer of 'Days of Our Lives', the long-running American soap. 'The statement we constantly get in our mail is, "Get them together" – whoever "them" happens to be at the moment. Conflict is good in the beginning but you hope the audience sees through the conflict and realises the two characters are meant for each other.'

But kinships are what really hold the soaps together. Romance, friendships, marriages might disintegrate but families last, hopefully, forever. Of course the reason so many romances and even marriages go off the rails in soaps is simply because the writers must keep the interest of viewers. If every marriage was made in heaven the soap would become extremely predictable and boring – like many marriages! Because soaps move at a leisurely pace compared to other television drama which must be compressed into an hour, families have a chance to grow and develop. They can age, marry, have children, die. A classic example was the character played by Charita Bauer in the American soap 'The Guiding Light', who was on screen for thirty years and grew from a young bride into a grandmother. Viewers grew old with her.

Another important factor is the community. Mythical towns are created by writers or in the case of 'Neighbours', a mythical street. Whatever may happen to the characters, few changes take place in the community. In real life Australians tend to move out of their houses, restlessly searching for better places and classier neighbourhoods as their living standard improves. If they began moving *en masse* out of Ramsay Street there would not be a 'Neighbours'.

In making soaps, certain techniques are used over and over again, the telephone for example. The telephone is the soap opera's most useful instrument because, above all, it allows the talk to continue even if only one character is on screen – and talk is what soaps are all about. Should a character for some reason be absent, the actor or actress off sick, for instance, the telephone can always ring with the character on the other end of the line. A quick rewrite can mean the basic storyline need not be broken.

Another handy gadget is the doorbell. If a scene needs to be cut suddenly, the doorbell can ring. At the same time the expressions on the faces of those on camera i.e. fear, happiness, embarrassment, can indicate what may happen in future scenes. The doorbell is also a splendid prop for a cliffhanger: illicit lovers are at it. The bell jangles.

*A very public breakfast. 'Neighbours' stars Myra de Groot,
Anne Haddy, Alan Dale and Stefan Dennis promote the series*
(Photo: News Ltd)

Their faces freeze. The credits roll. Without the doorbell, writers would have problems, another reason for confining soaps to indoors. There are not a lot of doorbells down the back paddock.

Cameras are used carefully to portray certain scenes. A widely used technique is the eye-level camera angle. High or low angles are sometimes utilised but only to make a special point. For instance, a camera pulling back often means we are about to leave the soap opera world. The eye-level camera helps create the illusion we are looking at one character from the eye level of another, that we are in the lounge or the bar involved in the action.

Such matters as the time of day are easily portrayed on soaps. 'Neighbours' uses the simple method of having plenty of exterior shots in the can, taken during various times of the day or night. A quick glimpse of a house at night before cutting to an interior scene establishes the scene is set after the sun has gone down. Likewise, a soft morning shot with a few birds twittering in the background establishes the household is stirring for the day.

These 'tricks' create an illusion of reality. So involved do people become in soaps, so familiar are the characters, that often the difference between fact and fiction is blurred. Jenny Young, who played a runaway girl in the early days of 'Neighbours', was accosted in the street by an elderly woman who thought Jenny should return immediately to her parents. 'I was shopping one day when a grandmother attacked me with her handbag,' Jenny recalled. 'She kept yelling at me and saying, "Go home to your parents, you naughty girl."'

If for some reason a soap does not appear at its regular time, fans often feel their lives have been drastically altered. A vacuum suddenly appears. They become extremely irritable like a drunk without drink or commuters when the regular train fails to arrive. Should the day come when a madman presses the button that unleashes nuclear war, it had better not happen when 'Neighbours' is screening. The three-minute warning would just have to wait until Charlene and Scott resolved their particular problems of the day.

3

'Neighbours' - Early Days

Ian Holmes sat back in his office chair and thought about soap operas. They often occupied his mind because as president and managing director of the television production company, Grundy Organisation, his main job was overseeing the making of soaps and game shows, but mostly soaps. The company had been in operation since 1959 when its founder, Reg Grundy, introduced 'Wheel of Fortune' to television, a programme with a format which is still running in a revamped version in Australia today.

Few people knew more about the business of soaps than Holmes. In 1973 he was appointed programme director of Channel 10, in Sydney, and three years later was the general manager. Only recently established, Channel 10 was lagging badly behind its two commercial rivals. Holmes believed nothing but a soap could save the station. At the back of his mind was an idea for a soap, or a serial drama as they preferred to call it, set in a block of flats. He discussed the idea with producers Don Cash and Bill Harmon, suggested the script should be kept spicy – and 'Number 96' was born. Even its title had sexual connotations. The next inspiration he had was to run it five nights a week. Originally 'Number 96' was to go out only one night a week but Holmes insisted it should be stripped across the five days.

'"Number 96" was initially quite different from anything the viewer had seen before and, to increase its impact, the storylines were controversial,' Holmes told *Sydney Morning Herald* writer, Tim Cribb. 'It was programmed every week night in prime time which hadn't been done before. It was also quite expensive to begin with. In all those ways it was quite a gamble ... "Number 96" acted as a catalyst. The sort of characters it exposed on television hadn't been previously used. They were controversial, but if the community was not ready to see that subject matter and those characters, they would have rejected it. It was a catalyst that brought certain subjects into much more open discussion, both in public and in the home.'

Channel 10's publicity chief, Tom Greer, organised a skilful promotional campaign, promoting the première episode as the night television lost its virginity. In no time at all it was topping the ratings, some nights attracting half the Australian television audience. Pubs complained customers went home early to watch it rather than having another drink or three and restaurants said diners bolted down their meals at indigestion pace so as not to miss it. It went into television mythology as the soap that saved a station, its popularity allowing Channel 10 to pay off several million dollars of its debt and firmly establish itself. 'Number 96' ended in 1977.

Holmes then moved to the Grundy Organisation where he helped plan and launch a number of soaps, including 'Prisoner', which became a cult show in the United States, 'Sons and Daughters' and 'The Young Doctors', both screened in Britain, 'The Restless Years', 'Waterloo Station', 'Starting Out' and 'Taurus Rising'. Some worked, others didn't. 'The difficulty in this business is that when you think you know what's going to happen, you really don't. It's entirely unpredictable,' Holmes said.

In 1984 Ian Holmes was thinking of soaps. So was Reg Watson, head of TV Drama at the Grundy Organisation. Born and raised in Brisbane, Watson went, like so many creative Australians, to Britain because of the work limitations at home. He set up ATV's first game show, 'Hit the Limit', wrote early episodes of 'Emergency Ward 10', then worked for several years on 'Crossroads'. Always in his mind was the idea of a serial like 'Neighbours'.

'I first got the idea for "Neighbours" in England watching "Coronation Street",' he said. 'I spent long enough in England to know that "Neighbours" was just right for viewers over there too.'

In fact Holmes and Watson (that duo has a familiar ring) were so confident it would be a success in Britain they wanted to coproduce it with the BBC and include several English characters. 'But that was scrapped when the BBC failed to get its daytime schedule together by the time we were ready to go with "Neighbours",' said Holmes.

Watson was originally going to call the soap 'No Through Road' or 'One Way Street'. 'In the end it came down to being what it is, a story around neighbours,' said Watson. 'Anything that happens in an average street will happen in this serial. I came to the conclusion that the "heavy" in neighbours is life itself, and once you accept that, it opens up everything – that's the one "heavy" we face from the day we are born. The show's simplicity is where its strength is. The "Neighbours" format was hard to get right because of its simplicity. I rewrote the first episodes twenty times.'

Keeping in mind the need to stay away from violence, mayhem and murder, the basic ingredients of many soaps, Watson portrayed Ramsay Street as a bright place with handsome young people scattered among the older folk, their problems as mundane as barking dogs or a toothache. 'I wanted to show three families living in a small street in a Melbourne suburb, who are friends. Humour was to play a big part in it and the other important thing was to show young people communicating with older people. The characters will make mistakes. Quite often people do silly things and make stupid mistakes in their lives.'

But more importantly the script had to stay within the bounds of suburban credibility. 'There is a point beyond which you don't go and that is where you get into the sensational aspects that really don't apply to the majority of people. So you pull it back and keep it real and entertaining.'

Ian Holmes liked Watson's idea, especially the way 'Neighbours' responded to the everyday problems confronting the average Australian family. 'Those everyday problems that loom large in our lives range from changes wrought by a 15-year-old daughter going through the sometimes emotional experience of becoming a woman to other situations of more regular types such as the happiness that pervades a family when they simply buy a dog,' said Holmes.

The Seven Network gave the go-ahead. Production began in Melbourne, a city many consider a funny place to produce anything outside a decent bout of influenza. 'If you want to get ahead in Melbourne, you should go to Sydney,' said one critic. Melbourne was once the centre for home-grown drama but many of the artistic types moved north to Sydney which became the location for much of the television and film production. Melbourne was chosen for 'Neighbours' because studio space was available.

The Seven Network outlayed $A8 million for the first year of 'Neighbours'. Great care was taken with the auditions, the actors given only a thumbnail sketch of their characters even after signing for their roles.

Watson sat them down and got them to talk about how they were going to play their parts. He was looking for actors who resembled not so much the average neighbour, but the kind of neighbour most people would like to have. He didn't want plain, ordinary neighbours, normal neighbours if you like. In this he echoed the wisdom of actor Vincent Price, who once observed: 'One of the deaths of Hollywood is that they tried to make everyone look normal. Some of the actresses who are around today look and sound like my niece in Scarsdale. I love my niece in Scarsdale, but I wouldn't pay to see her act.' Great secrecy surrounded the production because television programming is war and the Seven Network wasn't about to let its opponents know its plans for the 1985 ratings offensive.

The outside world became aware of 'Neighbours' when Estelle Bauer peered through her lounge window to see a man taking Polaroid pictures of her house. She thought it somewhat curious because although her house was a pleasant enough place, it wasn't Blenheim Palace. She forgot about the incident until three weeks later when the man returned, knocked on her door and asked permission to use her house in a new television series.

'You're pulling my leg,' said Mrs Bauer.

The man, a location scout for 'Neighbours', convinced her he had no intention of doing any such thing, then went on to visit Mrs Bauer's neighbours, the Aldingers and the Pierces, seeking the same permission. Being good neighbours, they met a few days later in the Aldingers' backyard to discuss the proposition.

'We all decided to give it a go,' said Helga Aldinger. 'The nice thing is that we all get on so well together. All our neighbours are marvellous.'

The three comfortable, middle-class homes became the residences of the denizens of Ramsay Street. The real street is a quiet cul-de-sac not far from the scenic but fire-prone Dandenong Ranges in Vermont South, a suburb lying in the 'brick and Volvo' belt of Melbourne. The street, or the Court as residents call it, was not the production company's first choice because the homes were considered a little too upmarket. But there were advantages that outweighed the problems, namely the quietness of the street, the fact that there were few homes built there and there was rear access where heavy vehicles could be parked out of camera range.

After the neighbourhood meeting, the residents signed contracts with the Grundy Organisation for regular payments, not substantial but said to be enough to help pay off the mortgages. Then they waited to see what making a soap was all about.

What it was all about was inconvenience. A few weeks later outside broadcast vans, lighting trucks, a catering unit, cars, an old bus used for make-up and wardrobe and about a hundred cast and crew moved into the street, thick black cables snaking across carefully mown lawns, lights glaring in the middle of the day. 'I came home one day and found graffiti all over my garage doors,' said Mrs Bauer. 'I was horrified at first, but it was okay. They used washable pink hair spray and they rinsed it off with a hose.'

The residents of the Court soon learned to live with problems they couldn't have imagined before. The Court was used up to three days a week, most of the action taking place on the driveways, yards and footpaths.

Residents were sent the filming schedule so they could plan their movements. And plan they had to. They couldn't suddenly paint their houses, do renovations, add an extra storey, plant new trees or even lop one without consulting the Grundy Organisation. Mowing the lawn and gardening had to be fitted into the shooting schedule. When taping was under way, the residents stayed behind discreetly drawn drapes and blinds, the children played elsewhere or kept down their voices if they played in their own backyards. Even visitors had to telephone beforehand to check that their arrival didn't interfere with the schedule of 'Neighbours'.

The location was kept secret but it's not easy disguising the vehicles and people required for each shoot, especially once the street had become the most famous suburban thoroughfare in the country. Word soon spread and matters became a little messy. At five o'clock one Sunday morning a brick was thrown through the window of one house, waking families and terrifying young children. Police were called and according to one newspaper 'the tiny street looked more like a scene from "Miami Vice" than the friendly "Neighbours"'.

Children invaded the street on their way home from school, drunken louts roared along it in their cars, letter boxes were stolen from front gardens as souvenirs and pot plants taken. The *Sun-Herald* newspaper reported an interview with one resident who, on the advice of police, asked for her name not be published. 'One of the residents in the street is a police officer and we have called him in for a discussion about our welfare. He has recommended we band together and shun any identification of our street in the media. So far the press have been very co-operative but any further reference will only incite more violence or vandalism. It may be too late, as everyone seems to know the location.

'This street was once very quiet. We do not blame the crew or cast of "Neighbours" in any way as they are all very friendly … People even ring up in the middle of the night to ask if "Neighbours" is being filmed the next day. Going on to an unlisted number will cause huge interruption to our family, our social lives and to our business. We think the TV life of "Neighbours" will probably be prolonged, as it is one of the very few shows being made in Melbourne. Family nerves are being tested and we have fears for the young children with the traffic and non-stop flow of strangers. Who'd want to buy a house and live in Australia's best-known street with the inconvenience and violence that has now become part of it?'

Who indeed! Filming still takes place in the Court even when the weather is as lousy as only Melbourne weather can be. There is a joke that in Melbourne you can get the four seasons in one day, except it's not funny. Jenny Stevens, in the *Sun-Herald*, described the scene in the Court on a day typical of Melbourne, be it summer or winter: 'If it's cold and miserable with a steady drizzle turning garden beds underfoot to a sticky, black squelch, the show must still go on, rain or not. Boots, sheepskin and 'driza bone' coats, leg warmers and umbrellas are on hand. If the script calls for washing to be put on the line, the prop

Early stars in the series: Max and Maria Ramsay (played by Francis Bell and Dasha Blahova)

department washing goes on, rain or not. On and off at least eight times until the actors and cameramen get it right.

'In the TV script, Ramsay Street doesn't have strict seasons. If the autumn trees are dropping leaves, the garden is bare, and the script needs Mrs Daniels to cut flowers, the problem is solved by having the actress disappear around the corner and return with a bunch bought by the ubiquitous prop department . . .'

Another problem for the cast, or at least the younger members, is that they're required to sit around backyard swimming pools showing their muscles, or lack of them as the case may be. This is an important part of 'Neighbours' – lots of good-looking young people, the embodiments of youth, health and vitality. But because of the weather, Melbourne, like Manchester, is not a great city for swimming pools, whereas Sydney, as seen from an aircraft, seems to have a patch of blue in every second backyard. If the script calls for a swimming-pool scene, no matter what the weather, the actors have to play the parts. Fortunately some swimming-pool scenes can be shot indoors.

Then there are the interiors. Because much of the action in a soap takes place indoors, the interiors are more important than the exteriors. Viewers come to know every ornament, every cushion. They have to be unobtrusive, comfortable and familiar like an old slipper or a picture that has been hanging for years.

'It's like background music,' says art director, Ken Goodman, 'simply there to create the atmosphere.' Stephen Keller, set designer for 'Neighbours', tried for a carefully designed mess, piles of well-thumbed magazines, dirty dishes in the sink, notes stuck on the refrigerator door, the bits and pieces of daily life in the suburbs. 'I want the rooms to be busy, to feel as if they're lived in by real people,' says Keller.

'Neighbours' went to air on the Seven Network on 18 March 1985, in the 5.30pm time-slot, a bold move for a soap. Research by Seven discovered what it believed was a new audience the network had not attracted before, sitting at home early in the evening desperate to be entertained by more than cartoons or game shows, the usual fare at that hour. Optimism was high, the future looked good. As producer John Holmes, who moved to 'Neighbours' from 'Sons and Daughters', said, 'I feel more confident with "Neighbours" than I did with "Sons and Daughters".'

And as actor Peter O'Brien (Shane) said, 'It's great to think I could be in a long-running series.'

However, as the months passed, the executives of Seven Network looked at the ratings figures with feelings of extreme discomfort. They were seeing signals they would rather not. 'Neighbours' was performing well in Melbourne and doing reasonable business in Brisbane but in Sydney, the country's biggest market, it wasn't drawing flies. Rumours spread among the cast. 'We heard them but we didn't really believe them,' said Peter O'Brien. 'We had heard it all before.'

One evening, seven months after 'Neighbours' began, O'Brien was having a beer in a Melbourne pub. Two television executives were standing near him, unaware he was within earshot.

'They don't know it yet, but we're here to axe their show,' one executive said.

O'Brien all but choked on his beer. Early next morning he telephoned a producer.

'What's this about the show going?' he inquired.

'No, there's nothing in it, just a rumour,' said the producer. At that moment the producer's phone rang. It was from head office and the message was: 'Neighbours' is finished.

4

Success on Channel 10

The headlines in Australia were of the size one might expect for World War Three. TOP TV SOAPIE AXED! screamed the front page of the Sydney *Daily Mirror*, the story going on to say the Australian television industry was in financial turmoil following the announcement that 'Neighbours' was history. The newspaper quoted 'Neighbours' producer, John Holmes: 'For the first time in Australian TV, shows are being axed because of money and not because of ratings ... It's not the ratings any more, it's plain dollars and cents.'

While this was true, it was nothing new for a show to be axed for financial reasons. Most were. If they couldn't pay their way they were out of the door faster than an unwanted salesman. But Ian Holmes, head of the Grundy Organisation, wasn't bothering with newspaper headlines. He was tying up the switchboard calling various people, not least the bosses of the Ten Network. 'They were astonished to hear from me,' he said.

Holmes put to them the idea they should pick up 'Neighbours'. For a series to swap channels was hitherto unknown in Australia though not uncommon in the United States ('Hill Street Blues' being a prime example). Bosses at the Ten Network had a lot of faith in Holmes and their own ability to make the soap work, although it was recognised some of the format had to be changed, as well as a few characters, and humour injected. 'Forty per cent of the content was to be sit-com based,' said Grundy executive Peter Pinne. The Ten Network liked the idea, a deal was sealed.

Because the Seven Network had many episodes in the can, it was

Scott and Charlene – the romance of the decade (Jason Donovan and Kylie Minogue)

The original cast of 'Neighbours'. From left to right: Julie Robinson (Vikki Blanche), Scott Robinson (originally played by Darius Perkins), Helen Daniels (Anne Haddy), Lucy Robinson (Kylie Flinker), Paul Robinson (Stefan Dennis), Jim Robinson (Alan Dale), Danny Ramsay (David Clencie), Des Clarke (Paul Keane), Daphne Lawrence (Elaine Smith), Shane Ramsay (Peter O'Brien), Maria Ramsay (Dasha Blahova) and Max Ramsay (Francis Bell)

Alan Dale who plays Jim Robinson with Sascha Close who took over from Kylie Flinker as his screen daughter Lucy

In the end it was Des Clarke (Paul Keane) who won the hand of Daphne Lawrence played by the Scottish-born Elaine Smith

Robinson father and son with Zoe (Jason Donovan, Ally Fowler and Alan Dale)

A DAY AT THE RACES

Above left: Alan Dale reads the form at the Melbourne Cup races

Above right: Stefan Dennis (who plays Paul Robinson) with his wife, Australian model Roz

Right: Anne Haddy (who plays Helen Daniels) with husband James Condon, who appeared in 'Neighbours' as Douglas Blake

Jason and Kylie enjoying the sun at Fremantle, home of Australia's America's Cup Challenge

Danny Ramsay – played by David Clencie

*The 'Neighbours' girls have a day off –
Elaine Smith, Kylie Minogue and
Annie Jones*

*And the 'Neighbours' boys have a day
off in the bush – Jason Donovan and
Guy Pearce*

Kylie takes a look at beautiful Portsea beach – helped by the surf patrol of the Portsea Life Saving Club

Peter O'Brien (Shane Ramsay) may be a soap star but he isn't above rolling up his sleeves in the kitchen

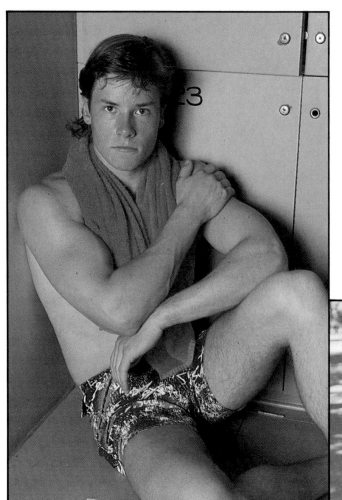

*Ex body builder champ
and sports fanatic Guy Pearce*

*The first Lucy Robinson –
played by Kylie Flinker*

still screening 'Neighbours'. 'Seven was furious with the deal we made,' said Ian Holmes. 'It was still airing a serial it was killing, and we were winning publicity for a rival channel.'

The reason for its failure on the Seven Network was blamed, mostly, on its 5.30pm time-slot in Sydney. In Brisbane and Melbourne, where it was more successful, it was screened at 6pm, but in Sydney that was news time. 'With such an early time-slot it picked up a young following, but not a huge following, not large enough to sustain the cost of Australian drama,' said producer Phil East.

John Holmes agreed. 'People who would have enjoyed the programme were either not home from work or were busy tending to children,' he said. 'Of course I was disappointed when it was axed. It did not appear to get a fair go. I don't know if "Neighbours" with a different time-slot would have fared better on Seven. All I know is that a programme is only as good as its opposition.'

Peter Pinne thought one of the reasons for its early failure was that Seven had too many soaps, the network also screening 'A Country Practice' and 'Sons and Daughters'. 'They couldn't sustain all three so they cancelled "Neighbours" after 171 episodes,' he said, adding that when Ten bought the series 'Channel Seven were so outraged we're told they burned all the "Neighbours" sets'.

In planning the new season of 'Neighbours' in its new home, the Grundy Organisation had to remove many of those actors whom it thought didn't measure up to standards. Darius Perkins was a person-able young man who joined 'Neighbours' at the beginning in the role of Scott Robinson. Aged twenty, he was no stranger to television, having won an award for best new talent for the mini-series, 'All The Rivers Run', and starred in the tele-movie 'Matthew and Son'. Popular with viewers, he was considered a 'good sort' by female fans but when contracts were signed after the Ten Network takeover, his signature was not required. He was replaced by Jason Donovan. 'I blew it,' he confessed. 'I was too young and inexperienced to handle it.'

What happened to Perkins could be a warning for any young soap actor. They join a series and within a few months are big fishes, especially in the relatively small pond of Australian television. Everyone wants to know them, they have more friends than they thought possible, are pursued by the opposite sex, in some cases, by the same sex, greeted as old mates by people they have never seen before, are invited to all the best parties, their heads balloon and they believe they are big stars. Pressures mount.

'Unless you've done it and had to cope with the pressures you can't understand,' said Perkins. 'The whole thing of losing your identity – people actually believe you are Scott and girls are constantly coming up to you in the street. The whole publicity hype is hard. You feel isolated in a way, up on another level, a bit untouchable, a bit alone. But, still, that is absolutely no excuse for how stupid I was. The whole thing freaked me out completely. When my girlfriend and I used to go out, girls were unbelievable in the streets. It puts a huge strain on any relationship you had. We used to have the most incredible fights about other girls and it really upset me.'

He said he had heard that stories were told that he was unco-operative and late for work, both cardinal sins in the hard grind of churning out five episodes of soap a week. 'I don't think I was ever unco-operative. I might have been late a couple of times. I didn't understand then how much money it cost if they were held up. I should've known better. What was lacking was a professional attitude.'

After leaving 'Neighbours' he couldn't get a job on television and instead he worked for a while as a picture framer, his telephone, an actor's lifeline, disconnected for not paying the bill. 'When I went for an interview, you could see what they were thinking: "Is he stoned?"' It was eighteen months before Perkins worked again on television, in a guest role on 'The Flying Doctors'.

Darius Perkins' case is not rare in television, especially in soaps. Success has ruined bigger stars than ever came out of the soap industry. Perhaps they should remember the words of Spencer Tracy who put the entire business into perspective when he said, 'Why do actors think they're so goddam important? They're not. Acting is not an important job in the scheme of things. Plumbing is.'

Kylie Minogue appears to understand better than many the fleet-ingness of fame. She told Shona Martyn, of *Good Weekend Magazine*, 'I don't think you can get too comfortable with where you are because you could be a nobody tomorrow. I'm just enjoying things at the moment and so when I'm tired and think, I don't want to do this any more, I wish I worked nine-to-five, I just think that it might not be here

Darius Perkins, who was the original Scott Robinson, with Vikki Blanche and Paul Keane

in a few months and that there's probably a million people who would kill to be where I am. I've just been very lucky.'

Peter O'Brien, who quit 'Neighbours' when he decided he'd had enough, not only of soap fame and getting his shirt torn off every time he made a public appearance, but of the daily toil, said he felt sorry for young actors who came from nowhere and went straight into 'Neighbours' to become, in a few months, household names. 'They're starting to expect the world,' he said, 'and I don't know what they'll do when all this finishes. They expect to get into nightclubs for nothing. They won't fly economy, only first class.'

Mrs Mangel (Vivean Gray) with Harry Henderson (Johnny Lockwood) at the Wedding of the Year (Photo: News Ltd)

As a producer, Tony Virgo, formerly with 'EastEnders', has seen the sour side of success, the fickleness of the public. 'When the stars of soaps first start work they are keen and energetic,' he said. 'Then all of a sudden they're being hailed as superstars and you can't go out and have a quiet meal with them without being badgered for autographs or mobbed by adoring fans. About 80 per cent of them then start to believe all their publicity and think they're the greatest thing since sliced bread. Usually when this starts happening they don't think they have to put any effort into their work any more and start making the most outrageous demands on their colleagues. They become monsters. The sad part about all this soapie adulation is that when a particular show folds, the actors are so typecast they have no hope of getting another decent role. I really don't know what they're going to do with themselves and their egos. It's a real problem and a shame.'

With 'Neighbours' placed into the more sensible hour of 7pm, the Ten Network pulled out all the publicity stops. 'Late last year letters and petitions from thousands of "Neighbours" fans poured into the offices of Grundy Productions,' blared expansive and expensive newspaper advertising. 'They were pleading for the return of their favourite drama series threatened with eviction by Network Seven. We at Network Ten know a good thing when we see it. Ten commissioned Grundy's to produce a new series of "Neighbours" for 1986. And we gave the popular drama series a brand new time-slot.' Not only did the advertisements tell the public what was happening, they also gave Ten the opportunity to sink the slipper into its rival, to use a once-fashionable Australian expression.

Posters went up. Newspaper journalists who wrote about television were wined and dined. Radio pumped out a stream of advertisements. Aircraft dragging banners droned over city beaches, disturbing the hot dreams of sunbathers. The management of the Ten Network sat back, reasonably confident it had done all it could to make 'Neighbours' the programme the entire country would be talking about.

People may have been talking, but unfortunately they were not watching. Three months after it was taken over by the Ten Network, 'Neighbours' once more faced the dreaded axe. The ratings showed it was geting only eight points at 7pm, four points lower than when Seven decided it was a loser in the 5.30pm slot.

George Brown, then managing director of Channel 10, Sydney, called the station's promotion chief, Brian Walsh, into his office. 'Walshie, we can't let this programme run much longer.'

'I think I can make it work,' said Walsh, 'just give me time.'

'Three weeks, then.'

'How about six?'

'All right, six weeks.'

Walsh was given a handsome budget of close to $A500,000 and let loose. A clever marketing man, Walsh has always held the belief there has to be a novelty factor and hook to every promotion, as he told Robin Oliver, of the *Sydney Morning Herald*: 'This is where I believe the other stations have fallen over. I got boo-hooed by the opposition for quite a lot of my promotions, but I found it interesting when they started copying.'

He put the cast to work. They were more than willing because at any given time there are more actors than acting roles and the unpleasant alternative to working before the cameras was waitressing, selling underpants in a department store or going on the dole. Some cast members had gone virtually from school into 'Neighbours'; they knew no other type of work. 'The cast was upset when the show was axed at Seven and they didn't want to lose it again,' said producer Phil East. 'They were determined to do anything to make "Neighbours" a success on its new home channel.'

One of Walsh's first promotional ideas was a campaign in which members of the public were asked to nominate local people for acts of outstanding good neighbourliness, prizes being television sets. Personalities from 'Neighbours' were flown to Sydney each weekend – the airfares and accommodation alone cost $A100,000 – to deliver dozens of television sets to nice neighbours all over Sydney. It worked well. Ratings climbed. 'I think it's a mistake to always go for the commonly drawn line of the print or electronic media when you're trying to sell to the consumer,' commented Walsh. 'You have to open up your areas of communication as wide as you possibly can.'

Bearing this in mind, Walsh used the huge Westfield shopping centres scattered through suburban Sydney which attract large crowds on Saturdays. 'It's like McDonald's,' explained Walsh. 'The greatest thing for a publicist is to get the tray mats at McDonald's, because you get a fantastic impact with everybody who sits down and eats off a tray. Westfields are the same. My opposite numbers at the other channels don't seem to realise that in any given week 1.5 million people go through Westfield centres in the Sydney metropolitan area. That to me is a media in itself. You can't ignore that. We dragged the cast around every shopping centre till their feet were bleeding. They were working 12-hour days on the set Monday to Friday ... They wanted to keep working and they gave and gave of their time.'

Walsh's strategy worked. 'Neighbours' never looked back. Millions of Australians began their serious viewing each weekday evening to the voice of Barry Crocker, who, incidentally, played the chunderous ocker in the movie, *The Adventures of Barry McKenzie,* singing the Tony Hatch–Jackie Trent theme song: 'Neighbours, everybody needs good neighbours. Just a friendly wave each morning, helps to make a better day ...'

But spare a sympathetic thought for the Seven Network executives who threw out 'Neighbours', thus joining such great show business legends as Dick Rowe, the agent who turned away the Beatles, or the characters in the music industry who advised a young Elvis Presley that as a singer he would make a good truck driver. Glen Kinging, Channel 7's (Sydney) programme director still turns shades of pink when reminded he once had 'Neighbours' in his grasp. 'If it wasn't for us, they [Ten Network] wouldn't have it,' he sighed. 'Of course it hurts like hell.'

Ron Casey was general manager of Channel 7 (Melbourne) when 'Neighbours' was tossed on the rubbish pile. 'Obviously my timing was a little out,' said Casey. 'But at the time putting more money into "Neighbours" would have been like betting for a place in a one-horse race. It's a nice enough show, I suppose, but for the life of me I can't understand why it's done so well in Britain.'

5

'Neighbours' Conquers Britain

The 'Neighbours' invasion of Britain began quietly on Monday, 27 October 1986. Six months earlier, at the Cannes international broadcasting market, Ian Holmes had sold it to the BBC which was looking for a cheap programme to fill a daytime spot. No one will reveal the price paid but it's unlikely to have been much more than a couple of thousand pounds an episode, if that. Holmes announced the sale with this discreetly worded press release: 'The BBC has purchased "Neighbours" for national telecast throughout their United Kingdom network. We understand they intend airing the drama in their new daytime schedule, five days a week. Naturally we are delighted that such a renowned organisation as the BBC has shown such confidence in our all-Australian production. "Neighbours" is now rating extremely well throughout Australia and gives every appearance of a long and happy life. The announcement of this major sale will give credence to its potential longevity.'

The time-slots chosen by the BBC were 1.30pm, with a repeat the following morning at 9.05. It attracted a typical audience of housewives, shift workers, the unemployed, people home sick and those simply bludging, to use a fine old Australian word sometimes heard in 'Neighbours', and there the BBC was quite content to leave it, a nice little filler but nothing to get excited about.

However, strange things were happening out there in viewerland, the audience growing much more rapidly than anyone could have dreamed and soon five to six million were watching the afternoon screening. Children were getting interested, in fact complaints came

The famous smile – which regularly adds thousands to readership figures whenever it appears on a magazine cover

from schools that pupils were arriving late because they stayed home to watch the morning episode. Working mothers couldn't see it either and they, along with others, demanded the BBC do something about it, and do it quickly.

Half a world away in Australia the cast was also receiving signals that 'Neighbours' was taking off, perhaps faster than any programme previously in Britain. British fan mail was arriving by the sackload at the Ten Network offices. 'All my letters are from viewers excited about my Scottish ancestry,' said Elaine Smith, at the time. 'They make quite a point about the fact I was born in Scotland and say they particularly like my character. They're all wonderful letters.'

The audience grew. Irate listeners telephoned and wrote to the BBC demanding 'Neighbours' be screened at a time when people were home, such as in the evening. Letters of praise went to the BBC's 'Points of View'. The tabloid press printed tales of the comings and goings of the inhabitants of Ramsay Street, or rather the actors who played them. Peter O'Brien and Elaine Smith, on a promotional trip to London, appeared on 'Wogan', with O'Brien shaking his head and saying, 'I'm completely stumped by the success.'

Realizing it had a winner in its stables, the BBC looked at ways of getting it to the barriers for the prime-time race. 'We knew "Neighbours" would be good, but never this good,' BBC Daytime chief, Roger Loughton, said in November 1987. 'Its success has taken everyone by surprise. We've had thousands of letters asking for an evening time for all those out at work during the day. And we have to listen to what the public wants.'

The decision was made to screen 'Neighbours' in the evening, at 5.35, as well as in its old lunchtime slot, beginning in January 1988. The soap immediately doubled its audience and by February the cheeky youngster, with 16.25 million viewers, had beaten the 28-year-old 'Coronation Street' and was not far behind 'EastEnders'. 'England has gone "Neighbours"-mad,' said Carol Millward, of the BBC press office.

The BBC's top ten in February were:

1.	EastEnders	24.35 million
2.	EastEnders	23.35
3.	Neighbours	16.25
4.	Neighbours	15.20
5.	Neighbours	15.00
6.	That's Life	14.65
7.	Neighbours	14.55
8.	Neighbours	14.50
9.	Holiday '88	13.40
10.	All Creatures Great and Small	12.95

Some argued the figures claimed for 'Neighbours' were not a true reflection of its audience. The total is obtained by adding the figures of the two screenings, the afternoon and evening. The largest showing for a single audience was around nine million in the evening.

Still, it was a fair enough audience, certainly the biggest for any Australian soap. Interestingly enough, it beat such glossy and expensive American imports as 'Santa Barbara', which, according to Barry Brown, of the BBC programming department, generated a mere half million viewers. If more proof was needed of its popularity one need only turn to the (London) *Sunday Mirror*.

Early in 1988 the newspaper ran a competition built around 'Neighbours' with winners given a trip to Melbourne to see the soap being made. The response stunned newspaper executives. More than a million entries were received in the first three days and twenty extra staff were put on to cope. It was one of the most successful newspaper promotions held in Britain.

There was widespread puzzlement over 'Neighbours'' popularity. Carol Millward thought it might be connected with the large number of Britons in Australia. 'English people have a lot of relatives in Australia and they look on "Neighbours" as a way of seeing how they are living,' said Millward. 'The programme doesn't show impossibly high living standards, as in "Dallas" or "Dynasty". "Neighbours" is pretty middle class. And it's also got some bronze and hunky men, which helps.'

Terry Pearson, lecturer on films and television at Glasgow University, was not concerned with bronze and hunky men but rather the so-called classlessness of 'Neighbours', the lack of disadvantaged, such as the poor, in the series. The classless society is one of the great Australian myths, perpetuated by successive governments so they won't feel embarrassed when the wealthy spend $A10 million or so on homes fronting Sydney Harbour while a couple of kilometres away the homeless sleep on the streets and 14-year-old boys and girls sell themselves for drugs, or a decent meal. The neat brick homes of Ramsay Street, with their comfortable, well-stuffed sofas and modern kitchens, would be envied by a great number of Australians. About 500,000 are on or near the poverty line.

'That [classlessness] might be true in terms of the Australian reality of class, but we would find it hard to believe there was not a working class operating and probably suffering somewhat,' Pearson said. 'We are looking at it from the viewpoint of Thatcher's Britain. It is true all the characters seem to be out of the same class. Money never seems to be a problem in Ramsay Street.

'Take Clive, the one who studies to be a doctor and decided not to practise. Money is never a problem to him and yet he never seems to have a proper job. If you had it competing with "EastEnders" it might attract a huge audience at first simply because it is quintessential soap opera but sooner or later there might be an audience reaction against the absence of a working class.'

The Australian *Sun-Herald* asked a number of Fleet Street newspaper critics to explain the 'Neighbours' phenomenon, if that were possible.

Geoffrey Phillips, of the *Evening Standard*, thought 'Neighbours' was 'perfectly crafted as television to Hoover by. It's the TV equivalent of a fruit gum. I can't for the life of me see why it's a success, except that everyone has a perfect suntan ... It must have some secret ingredient which gets the British TV viewer in. But I'm not in any way persuaded that I'm missing anything from my intellectual life by not watching "Neighbours".'

Moira Petty, of *Today,* put its success down to its simplicity. 'The characters are two-dimensional and the plots come thick and fast. The storylines don't last long, so if you don't like one, another will come along in a few days. It also shuns all social issues which the British soaps cover. It has no relationship to the outside world – it is totally escapist. You never see the characters at work unless it's essential to the plot. They're usually sitting in each other's kitchens. They never knock on doors, they just come in and sit down – which to us is amazing. The characters are so appalling you are horrified but hooked. They never change, whether they're blackmailed or shot by their wife.'

Hugh Hebert, of *The Guardian*, admitted to being puzzled by its success. 'I think it's something to do with a new daytime audience. There is a huge pool of unemployed and under-employed people and the daytime phenomenon is tapping into that market. "Neighbours" has been lucky enough to take off as that audience has grown. But it has a lighter touch than "EastEnders" or "Coronation Street", it doesn't have such deep social problems.'

Elaine Smith, born in Largs, Ayrshire, traces her Scottish ancestry

Phil Tusler, of the *Sun*, thought it wasn't a bad little show. 'I think in the middle of the winter it's great to see all the sun. Being on at 5.35, it's an absolute phenomenon. If it was in a prime slot like "EastEnders" we'd be less surprised. It's happened so quickly, it's caught us out. But it's very popular with the kids – nine out of ten kids watch it. House-wives watch it as well.'

Minette Marrin, of the *Daily Telegraph,* called 'Neighbours' 'a sermon in soaps ... a celebration of the contemporary Australian way.' She went on: '"Neighbours" is high-grade comfort viewing. Most of the characters are nice. Their stories hang together smoothly and no crisis is dwelt on for long without a little relief. Problems get resolved or move out of the story. If the people and their habitat and their clothes seem unnaturally clean, what else can you expect from soap. And if television is a contemporary pulpit, "Neighbours" seems to me a much better ongoing homily than most bought-in American or European soaps.'

Critics at *The Times* were unable to comment because they had never watched 'Neighbours'.

However, the most direct attack on 'Neighbours' came, not surpris-ingly, from people connected with 'EastEnders', also screened in Australia. Carried five days a week by the ABC, the Australian equivalent of the BBC, it ends each night at 7pm when 'Neighbours' is starting on the Ten Network. As far as ratings are concerned, 'East-Enders' does not perform well Down Under. No British soap has fared well in Australia, not even 'Coronation Street' which was screened for a while in the Seventies but taken off because of poor ratings. On the other hand the daytime soaps, such as 'Days of Our Lives', 'The Young and the Restless' and 'General Hospital', perform satisfactorily and 'Dallas' and 'Dynasty' had good ratings until viewers peered beneath the false tinsel and found only more tinsel.

'"Neighbours" is great escapist entertainment but really is a waste of time,' said Tony Virgo, former 'EastEnders' producer. 'I think it's silly to have a show which literally millions of people tune into every day that doesn't relate to real-life experiences, whether they be contro-versial or not ... I think a main ingredient of their [Australian soaps] appeal to English audiences is the fact that they display an almost different type of culture – a breakaway from the stale English environ-ment.'

Linda Davidson, who plays the punk Mary in 'EastEnders', wasn't too keen on 'Neighbours' either, saying 'production was poor and the scripts appalling'. She said it was clear why 'nobody claimed the credit for writing the show. No one would be game to when the actors have to utter such banalities as "young love, isn't it grand".'

Wendy Jane Walker, who played Susan Barlow in 'Coronation Street', thought 'Neighbours' was a reasonable slice of escapist entertainment. It would be churlish to suggest she was pleased to see her old series get its come-uppance at the hands of 'Neighbours', but it's no secret she was less than pleased over the way she was written out of 'Coronation Street', her character having an abortion against the wishes of her husband. Because she was deeply involved in Britain's oldest soap, her opinions are worth considering.

'It's addictive,' she said of 'Neighbours'. 'I think it beats British and glossy American soaps hands-down. It's very much like "Coronation Street" was – years ago. It's about people, their relationships, squabbles and their ups and downs. You can identify with the characters as real people. Often literally nothing happens. Or rather nothing out of the ordinary. It's just people coping with the everyday problems of life, like burning the dinner. I think that appeals to viewers. You can escape from your own worries by watching someone else living them on screen.'

6

On the Sets of Ramsay Street

A taxidriver was giving his opinion of Kylie Minogue. 'If you ask me, they're working her much too hard,' he said. 'Picked her up the other day from the airport. She was so exhausted she just curled up in the back like a baby ...'

The 'Neighbours' cast works the sort of hours that would have some trade union bosses threatening to call a strike. Kylie is often required at the studio at 6.45am and in many interviews has spoken of her tiredness. Not only does she do a twelve-hour day on the soap but has lines to learn in the evenings and weekends are given over to publicity outings, signing autographs, talking to the press, being photographed from every angle and being displayed at shopping centres.

Almost everyone in 'Neighbours' complains of exhaustion. 'It's very hard work and very draining doing two and a half hours of drama a week,' said Francis Bell.

Darius Perkins thought it would be a reasonably easy task to play the role of Scott Robinson. 'I was used to getting a script, having time to get it all down, rehearse, all that,' he said. 'Suddenly the end of the week would come and this great pile of scripts would arrive. There was no time for anything except work. I was really very, very tired a lot of the time.'

Three days a week, Tuesday, Wednesday and Thursday, are spent taping, with rehearsals on Monday and Friday. Make-up is ready for its first customers at 6.30am, sometimes work is still in progress at eight o'clock at night. Helen Withers, of the now-defunct Sydney afternoon newspaper, the *Sun*, spent a day on the set and and gave this rundown on more than twelve hours in the studio:

6.30am.   Make-up, hairdressing, wardrobe and technical departments arrive (if a major set change is required, some of the crew may arrive at 4am).

6.45am.   First cast member is called, in this case it's Elaine Smith who plays Daphne Clarke.

7.00am.   Floor manager Alan Williamson and audio, video tape, lighting and camera crews arrive.

7.30am.   Taping starts for the first scene on the set of the Clarke house with Elaine, Paul Keane (Des Clarke) and Guy Pearce (Mike Young).

8.30am.   Action moves from the Clarke house to the Mangel set.

9.00am.   Annie Jones (Jane Harris) arrives in the 'Neighbours' 'resting' room from the make-up department.

9.30am.   In the studio, Myra de Groot (Eileen Clarke), Vivean Gray (Mrs Mangel) and Ian Smith (Harold Bishop) have stopped to watch a playback of a scene just taped. The next scene calls for a change of camera angles, and two crew members quickly roll up a carpet and move Mrs Mangel's television.

10.15am.   Laughter in the studio as Myra and Ian discuss a movie they had both seen on television the night before.

11.00am.   It's sit and wait for the cast – Myra uses this halt to give Vivean a quick lesson in the art of embroidery.

11.15am.   On set playing the prim and easily horrified Eileen Clarke, Myra lapses out of her conservative character and says: 'Jesus she's such a frigid cow, this old bird.'

11.30am.   Upstairs, director Paul Moloney sits in the darkened control room where he and five other technical and directing staff monitor the action down in the studio.

11.45am.   Banks of television monitors in the control room show what is happening in the studio, and on rival television stations and editing in the news room.

11.50am.   The last scene before lunch – Vivean stashes her scripts under one of Mrs Mangel's cushions before taping begins.

1.40pm.   After lunch hairdresser David Vawser and make-up artist Lois Jorgensen transform Anne Charleston into Madge Ramsay.

1.50pm.   Back in the studio, Annie Jones sorts through her character's record selection on Mrs Mangel's living room floor.

3.50pm. Action moves from the Mangel living room to the Ramsay house.

4.00pm. The Ramsay family of Anne Charleston, Craig McLachlan (Henry Ramsay), Jason Donovan (Scott Robinson) and Kylie Minogue (Charlene Robinson) start reading through their lines for the scene about to be taped. Director Paul Moloney comes down from the control room to discuss the scene, which will move across from the Ramsay kitchen to living room.

7.15pm. Six scenes later, taping has finally finished in the Ramsay home.

Gruelling though this schedule sounds, conditions of work and pay for the 'Neighbours' cast are, in fact, by no means harsh or unusual for a daily Australian soap – where time and money are at a premium. The Grundy Organisation, like any other production company, is on a tight budget and has much more limited resources than many British or American prime-time production companies.

Many will privately say that for the hours they put in, not only in the studio but on the publicity rounds, the rewards are minuscule. Darius Perkins said that after working on 'Neighbours' for nine months, he felt a pay rise would be a nice gesture from management. Deciding to seek one, he talked it over with other cast members who agreed it was a good idea and said they would back him. 'When the time came, I stuck to what I wanted and the others all backed down,' he said. 'I know people say you're paid a lot of money. But we weren't paid heaps, I can tell you. Some weeks I lost more in tax than I took home.'

Even the actors who are now big international names hardly require an armoured truck to take home their pay. In February 1988 Kylie Minogue was reported to receive only $A300 an episode, but, happily, she could earn several thousands for a personal appearance at, say, a shopping centre. In the same month an unnamed spokesman for 'Neighbours' was quoted as saying: 'At about £100,000 a week for five episodes, we are the cheapest brand of soap you can buy, but we're also one of the most popular. "Dallas" can spend more than that for just a few minutes' filming, and even your "Crossroads" is expensive by comparison.' Alan Dale, reported to be the highest paid actor in

'Neighbours' move house. Back row from left: *Anne Haddy, Myra de Groot, James Condon*. Front row: *Alan Dale and Stefan Dennis*
(Photo: News Ltd)

*Not overpaid, but certainly hard workers. Members of the
'Neighbours' cast.* Back row from left: *Myra de Groot, Francis Bell,
Anne Charleston, Paul Keane, Elaine Smith, Kylie Flinker, Anne
Haddy, Peter O'Brien and Ally Fowler* (Photo: News Ltd)

'Neighbours' at a little over £1,000 a week, said that when the long
hours were taken into consideration 'we are paid a pittance compared
to the Americans'.

Nor are conditions ideal at the Nunawading studios where
'Neighbours' is shot, a low, sprawling building of no particular charm

in a monotonous Melbourne suburb. Space is limited, with actors forced to find comfort where they can. Anne Haddy found it in a shower cubicle, where she set up a small study with chair, typewriter and reading material. A Grundy executive poked his head in one day. Anne hoped he would say, 'My gosh, you need more room, don't you?' Instead, he peered at the space, smiled politely and said, 'That's a very cosy spot you have here.'

Complaints aside, 'Neighbours' bubbled along nicely in Australia in 1987, helped by astute marketing by Brian Walsh who targeted young people as the audience to have and to hold. 'A soap has to be the talk of the office, the classroom next day,' he said. 'I read the other day that one headmaster was having ten-minute TV discussion periods at the start of each day. You want your programme to be in that discussion, because then the kids who are not watching it will begin to think they are missing something.' In another promotion the Ten Network gave away a block of land to viewers who had to dig for a hidden title deed.

A clever gimmick was to throw in personalities for guest appearances who might appeal to kids. One was Warwick Capper, star forward of the Sydney Swans Australian Rules football team, a player noted as much for his long blonde hair and tight shorts as his undisputed ability on the field. 'I don't know if acting is for me because I was really nervous with all the cameras, lights and the top actors,' he mumbled after his scene was shot.

Another seemingly good coup was signing Fiona Coote, who by the age of seventeen had undergone two heart transplants and was much admired across the Australian land for her courage. At fourteen, a seemingly healthy girl living at Tamworth, a New South Wales country town, a good student, a keen athlete, she was unexpectedly diagnosed as suffering from cardiomyopathy, a form of disease affecting the heart muscle which can cause sudden death. A four-hour heart transplant at St Vincent's Hospital, Sydney, gave her hope for a new life, but it was short-lived. Her body began rejecting the new heart. Another transplant was performed, this time successfully, and Fiona's name became synonymous with the gameness shown by great athletes and bushrangers – or highwaymen – such as Ned Kelly.

In June 1987, she rehearsed her role at the Melbourne studios. 'I did a few plays at school but never thought about acting as a career,' she said. 'I think everyone – my doctors included – was quite surprised.'

Next morning she was to have taped the episode but overnight fell ill. Hoping it was little more than nerves, the producers postponed shooting for the morning, but when it became obvious she would not be well enough, her part, sadly, had to be recast.

The success of 'Neighbours' still confounded many. After all, the soap showed an unreal world where people could apparently leave their homes untended and their neighbours were friendly, helpful souls who had nothing but the good of the community at heart. This was no more than yearning for the good old days, often a strong theme in soaps. The neighbourliness of Ramsay Street might still exist in remote country towns, but in the cities of Australia your neighbour is more likely to belt you on the nose because your trees dropped leaves in his yard or aim a gun at your dog after it dug up a rosebed. Neighbours quarrel, neighbours fight, neighbours covet your possessions, neighbours sometimes kill. And the idea of leaving the door unlocked, even when you're at home, would be considered not only eccentric but crazy. (In the last six months of 1987 Sydney had 47,000 burglaries reported to police – and a large number that weren't.)

Still, the popularity of 'Neighbours' gave academics the opportunity to ponder its attractions. Academics enjoy dissecting the latest media fad until all the whys and wherefores are laid out like innards after an autopsy. Albert Moran, lecturer in media studies at Griffith University, Brisbane, thought much of the popularity was because of viewers' curiosity about their own real-life neighbours. 'It allows us to have a kind of legitimised interest in gossip and a legitimised interest in our neighbours,' he observed. 'It becomes quite snoopy in real life. The tempo and rhythm of "Neighbours" matches our own lives. It is on there every night, just when families assemble for tea, and that emphasises the familiarity. Because it is so regular, it becomes as satisfying as the news.'

Another professional media-watcher, Leslie Stern, from Murdoch University, Perth, pointed to the lack of realism in 'Neighbours' as one of its attractions. 'Certainly there is a kind of identification with the characters and lifestyles,' she said. 'But there are many differences. There is a lot more happening in a show like "Neighbours" than in our own lives. But realism is not everything. If "Neighbours" was completely realistic, the viewers would be watching the soapie characters sitting around watching television themselves – because that's what people do. In "Neighbours" we can project and play out our fantasies. And because it involves so many complicated and unusual relationships between people, the intensity of the characters' lives is an attraction. Most people don't know their neighbours that well.'

In the halls of learning soaps were no longer looked upon with distaste or with intellectual arrogance. 'People might say "Neighbours" is just commercial pap but to the people who actually watch them, it means a lot,' said Toby Miller, a sociologist at the University of New South Wales, Sydney. 'Soapies don't really reinforce stereotypes any more than other media and they've become more progressive in recent years. If a young woman on a soap opera goes out and gets a good technical job, women watching can think, "I could do that". Soapies can help show people that they have choices.'

Fine words, supportive words. But many Australians were watching 'Neighbours' for totally different reasons. They were switching on because of a slip of a girl and a handsome young fellow, who in a remarkably short time had become so well known you only had to call them by their first names for people to know their identities.

Their names were, of course, Kylie and Jason.

7

Kylie
'Most Popular Personality'

Over a two-week period early in 1988, a teenager of nineteen summers, in full-time show business for no more than three years, won five major Australian entertainment awards. The first was the Australian Rock Industry Award for the biggest selling single of the year. Then, in only one night, she picked up four television Logies ...

The 'Logies' are named after John Logie Baird, the British inventor of television. The Logies ceremony, held at a luxury Melbourne hotel, and televised live all over Australia, is what society writers like to call a glittering night. It's an interesting ceremony – not least because the guests are well wined and dined beforehand, especially wined, and what happens is not always in the script.

Personalities are imported from Britain and the United States to add a little razzmatazz to the proceedings (even if some are in the autumn of their career – like Mickey Rooney, a presenter at the 1988 ceremonies). The Logies may be sneered at by some purists but they are a lot more fun than the determinedly self-important ritual of the American Academy Awards held in the sober atmosphere of the Dorothy Chandler Pavilion. One year the Hollywood actor Michael Cole, of Mod Squad, dropped a four-letter word while handing over an award, another year a well-known Australian actor fell off the stage. Glenn Ford refused to sit with a prominent Australian politician he considered anti-American, John Wayne and William Conrad got involved in a belly-butting contest.

In the 1988 awards, the thirtieth, two Australian television personalities enlivened the evening by throwing punches at each other, one bruising his jaw, the other his knuckles, both their reputations. Organised by the mass-circulation magazine *TV Week,* the awards are voted for by readers. And at the 1988 ceremonies it was soon obvious it was going to be Kylie's night. The envelopes were opened and four times the announcement was made: 'And the winner is ... Kylie Minogue.'

She walked to the stage to pick up statuettes for Australia's Most Popular Television Personality, Australia's Most Popular Actress, the Most Popular Australian Music Video Award and Most Popular Personality in the State of Victoria. 'We'll have to rename them the Minogies,' someone quipped.

Clutching her awards, she left behind the whooping and hollering and downing of drinks and went to a hotel suite where she collapsed on the bed and wept. It was a combination of exhaustion, emotion, nerves and concern over the recent publication of photographs showing her topless on a beach. 'It just got too much for her,' a friend said. 'She was overwhelmed by it all. You've got to remember, she's just a kid.'

She may not be a kid but she is one of those phenomena produced every now and again by the entertainment industry, with no more or no less talent than other performers but who somehow touch a public nerve. They appear to come from almost nowhere and must wear, appropriately or not, the tag of overnight success, leaving critics scratching their heads and veteran performers wondering where they went wrong. Through no fault of their own they provoke jealousy which in turn stirs the rumour pot.

Yet it's the public who chooses them. In Kylie's case they chose her because of her girl-next-door image. She is everyone's favourite sister or daughter or niece. Sex appeal had nothing to do with it. Shona Martyn, in *Good Weekend* magazine, described her as 'diminutive and incredibly pale without make-up, her conversation is quiet and peppered with phrases such as "a typical kid thing to do" and theatrical jargon: "There wasn't a dry eye in the house" ... she is pleasant, polite and unpretentious. She has a great smile.'

Kylie joined 'Neighbours' in the first half of 1986 as Charlene Mitchell, who would rather be a motor mechanic than continue at school. It didn't take long for the public to respond to her and in turn she gave

*Terry Blamey, manager to one of the world's hottest celebrities –
Kylie Minogue* (Photo: News Ltd)

everything she had, gave and gave to the point of exhaustion. 'I can't
say no,' she said.

Aware of her public, she never refuses a request for a publicity
appearance and treats every fan with respect. She receives 1,000 fan
letters a week and instead of relaxing in the evening, sitting back to
watch television as her father, Ron, often suggests, she attends to the
letters, handwriting the person's name and signing each one. So
obliging, say her publicists and management people. So easy to work
with. Her concern is that the fans take up so much time she neglects
her friends. 'A friend of mine rang up the other night just after I got
home and I was too tired to talk to her because I had to be up at six the
next morning. I think she understood but I felt a bit guilty saying I

couldn't talk to her and that I'd ring her another time. It's a bit hard then.'

Her toothy smile has appeared on at least forty magazine covers, each time sending the circulation graph climbing. One Australian magazine puts on 40,000 extra readers when she is on the cover. No matter if the stories contain little more than was previously published. After all she is only nineteen and has not been carried along too many of life's currents. But those teeth still appear regularly on the newstands.

In fact, her teeth have been the cause of some comment, and have even been studied by a psychic. Simon Turnbull, who can apparently predict all sorts of astonishing things from gazing at molars, reported: 'Kylie has a strong smile which shows a strong character. She has a defensive quality about her, which tends to come across as vulnerability. Kylie's top teeth overlay firmly in front of her back teeth, which implies an armour-like sense of protection. She is cautious yet also shows a determination in her approach to life and work. (If your teeth overlay when you smile, it shows a sense of endurance as well.) The future looks fortunate for the "Neighbours" star. However, a divorce or separation around her, which may be a source of worry, will not go through. This should be resolved by October, though, and her health, no matter how strong her endurance, will require plenty of rest around October.'

Her health has been the subject of much speculation by the media, mainly because she is pencil thin and has difficutly keeping on weight, causing one publication to come out with the fashionable anorexia scare. 'I think they ran out of something to write,' she said, with irritation in her voice because it was one of the few articles that upset her.

One reason she is so thin is that she doesn't like eating. Weighing not much more than six stone, she looks the type one would like to take home to mother for a square meal. 'I don't care about food,' she said. 'I'm not interested in it. I survive on fruit, prawns and water. That's enough for me.' Her weight concerns her fans so much they keep sending pizzas and takeaway food to her home. But she's quite happy with her weight. 'I don't feel good when I think I look heavy.'

The long hours that leave her exhausted also show on her body and face, at one time causing her to collapse. Exhaustion is a subject she often raises. 'I'm sick with exhaustion,' she said on one occasion. Another time she said, 'I'm so tired when I finish work that all I want to do is stay home and make clothes ... All I do is work, work, work.'

Born in Melbourne on 28 May 1968 – 'I'm a Gemini so sometimes I'm outrageous and sometimes I'm very quiet' – she inherited some show business genes from her mother Carol, an amateur ballet dancer. 'Basically I was shy, a bit quiet,' said Carol. 'I never really had the drive or ambition to go any further. I entered a few eisteddfods and competitions and did the exams but that was as far as I went. I think it's a hard life but I loved it while I was doing it.' She had Kylie and her other daughter Danielle, three years younger than Kylie, learn the piano because 'it is something you have for life'.

Kylie had just finished primary school when her mother took her for an audition to Crawford Productions, then the biggest Australian producer of drama, for the role of Carla, the little Dutch girl in 'The Sullivans', a long-running soap opera of the World War Two years. She got the role, then appeared in 'Skyways', set around an airport, and as a local toughie in 'The Henderson Kids'. Giving up acting, albeit more a hobby than a serious task, she went back to school for her Higher School Certificate, a scrap of paper many kids hope will be an entrée to the adult world but which too often is nothing more than a ticket to the dole office. Then she was signed for 'Neighbours' as Charlene Mitchell, first for one week, then for thirteen weeks, and then a contract through to mid-1988.

Kylie explains Charlene and her appeal by saying, 'I suppose people like her because she is an average teenager growing up, having difficulties with her mother. She is a bit of a rebel and they probably relate to that, and while she has her problems she will always come out on top. I certainly don't fight with my mum like she does – we get along really well. Charlene is much more tomboyish and outspoken than I am. She will generally say what she thinks, which is a good thing. If Charlene had trouble she would punch someone, but I would just get flattened if anything like that happened to me.'

In her first year as Charlene she won a Silver Logie for Most Popular Actress. In a business where swollen heads grow like pumpkins fed too much manure, where egos inflate like dirigibles,

'We'll have to rename them "Minoguies"' – *Kylie, winner of four*
'Logie Awards' in 1988 (Photo: News Ltd)

Kylie retains a modesty that is touching. 'I am really grateful for what I'm doing', she told Patrice Fidgeon of *TV Week,* using a theme she has repeated in interview after interview. 'I have been very lucky going from school to a full-time job like this in a show which is very popular. You can lose yourself in all that publicity hype, but I realised early on that when it's all over, you only have yourself left. In the past eighteen months I have learned to hide the deepest me. I only show that to very, very close people. When I started in "Neighbours" I just felt grateful that I had found work. I wanted to be an actress but it had never been one of those burning ambitions you read about. I was in the right place at the right time. It's that simple. I don't think I'm anything special. I'm like everyone else. I have seen what happens to people who can't and don't cope with the pressure. It's possible to lose what you are.'

Now all this might sound impossibly corny, in fact not unlike dialogue from a soap opera. But it happens to be the way she is. There is nothing about her that suggests the star, for that is what she is to many in Australia and Britain, or that she will ever fall into the traps concealed everywhere in show business. She does not frequent discos until dawn. She is not easily irritated. She does not swan about in flash cars, until 1988 she was driving one that in her own words 'lets out smoke and needs a new engine'. She makes many of her clothes. She even lives at home with her mum and dad and her sister and brother, although she has bought an old house for an investment and renovates it when she finds time. 'I love living at home with my family. So many of my friends come from broken homes but we're really normal – it's Mum, Dad, three kids and a dog. You can just be your normal dag self.'

Careful with money, she will not buy, for instance, clothes she considers too expensive. 'So many of them are so expensive I refuse to buy them on principle. Many of them are so easy to make. I used to make a lot of my own clothes and it's a lot cheaper and you end up with something that's original.' Always conscious the bubble could burst – 'I know that in a year it could all be gone' – she ponders her good fortune almost with a feeling of guilt she had the lucky breaks while others got no further than the back-stage door. 'It's daunting. Why is it that I've had all the luck?'

Kylie's sister, Danielle, has also mapped out a career in show business, as a senior member of 'Young Talent Time', a television variety show that as its name suggests features young people. In fact when Danielle joined 'Young Talent Time' in 1983 Kylie was introduced as her sister. 'I didn't like it,' said Kylie, 'but I didn't hold it against her in any way.' Danielle says she is not jealous of her sister's astonishing success.

'We share a love of singing and music but I'm not trying to compete with her,' said Danielle. 'I want to do my own thing. We don't see a lot of her because our schedules clash really badly. I see her for about ten minutes a week. It's like, "Hi ... bye" in the door, out the door. If we are at home at the same time, we are usually both asleep. I'm a lot louder than Kylie. She's really quiet, and she's so shy with people. I like energetic things, like swimming. She's quieter, she enjoys sewing, things like that.' Soap producers are smart operators and it was inevitable that Danielle would be offered an appropriate contract. She signed in March 1988, for a drama series called 'All The Way', as well as a recording contract.

Another Minogue, Brendan, two years younger than Kylie, a trainee television cameraman, is not concerned about being between two well-known sisters. 'Tempers blow rarely round here,' he said. 'We look for signs of tiredness in each other, especially in Kylie and Danielle, and we keep away. The girls work really long hours. We can tell if someone's tired or been working hard and we get out from under their feet. From having two famous sisters I've seen this business at its worst. I've also seen the hours they put into it. The thing I've learned most from watching the girls is that whatever else you do it must come second to being a happy family.'

So Kylie continued with 'Neighbours', at times getting away from the heavy demands by joining in jam sessions with some of the 'Neighbours' cast and crew. 'She doesn't get her singing from me,' said her mother. 'I can't sing a note, I couldn't even sing in church. But my father's cousin was the head of the conservatorium in Wales.'

Kylie liked to sing the Sixties hit 'Locomotion', originally recorded by Little Eva and later covered in the Seventies by Grand Funk Railroad. A Melbourne company, Mushroom Records, heard of her singing efforts, liked the results and released 'Locomotion'. It took off better than anyone had dreamed. 'It's fantastic,' said Kylie. 'I have to keep pinching myself to believe it's happening.'

In October 1987, she was invited to London to cut a new single with British producers Mike Stock, Matt Aitken and Pete Waterman, the team behind the international successes of Bananarama, Mel and Kim and Samantha Fox. The result was 'I Should Be So Lucky'. The song didn't even bother hanging around the lower reaches of the British charts before it took off, literally rocketing to the top.

'Her prospects as a recording star are, in one word, enormous,' said Amanda Pelman, of Mushroom Records. 'When I first heard a demonstration tape of 'Locomotion' it looked like she had enormous potential. We are entirely committed to her as a recording star and she's got a great future. She has co-written some of the tracks on her album.'

Not everyone had the enthusiasm of Mushroom Records. Many of Australia's top radio stations would not play 'I Should Be So Lucky' for various reasons. 'We are concerned about having anyone switch off and the single, according to our research, has a high irritant factor,' said Stuart Matchett, music director of the Sydney station 2SM, adding that two bars of the song had the station's audience complaining about being given 'children's music'. Another Sydney station, 2Day FM, said it had received a largely negative reaction from audience research into the record.

The public had other opinions. Within a few weeks, 'I Should Be So Lucky' had sold half a million and gone platinum, as they say in the record business. Kylie just smiled and said, 'Life is just getting better and better.'

Returning to London in March 1988, for further recording work, Kylie committed the cardinal sin of ignoring the British media on her arrival at Heathrow Airport. Accompanied by two minders only slightly smaller than King Kong and wearing dark glasses, she was taken straight from Customs to a waiting Daimler and driven away.

Next morning she woke in her hotel to read the comments of Jean Rook, of the *Daily Express*. Rook reckoned Kylie risked becoming 'a burnt-out old crocodile handbag'. She said Kylie should take lessons from Joan Collins, of 'Dynasty', on how to look glamorous after long flights, adding, 'Maybe getting off a plane looking as if you've just crawled out of a kangaroo's pouch is Australian style. "Neighbours" actress Kylie Minogue's disappointing arrival at Heathrow was worse

Kylie Minogue – Australia's Most Popular Personality

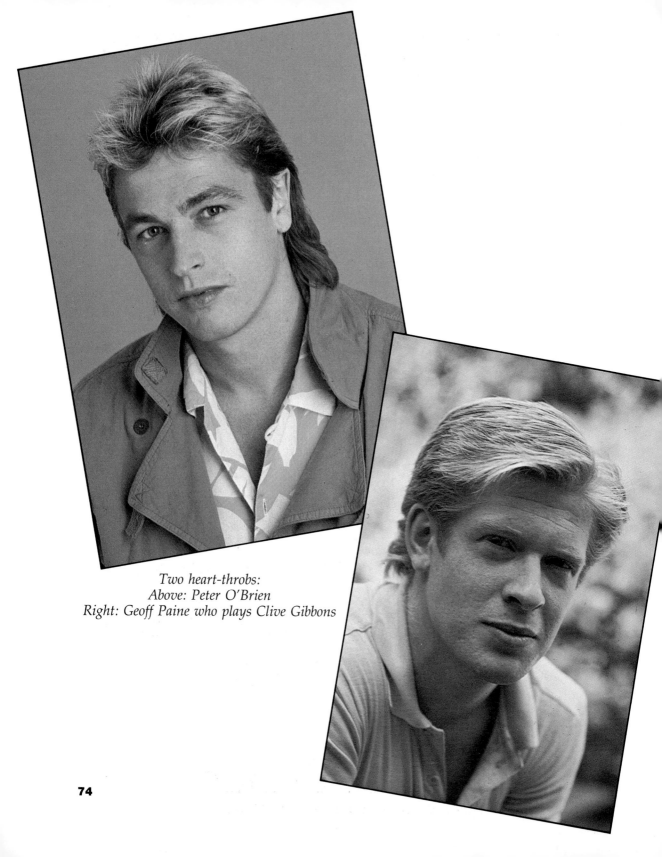

Two heart-throbs:
Above: Peter O'Brien
Right: Geoff Paine who plays Clive Gibbons

74

Kylie and friend during a break from filming

THE WEDDING OF THE YEAR!

Above: Charlene and Scott cut the cake

Left: Scott with best man Mike Young
(Guy Pearce)

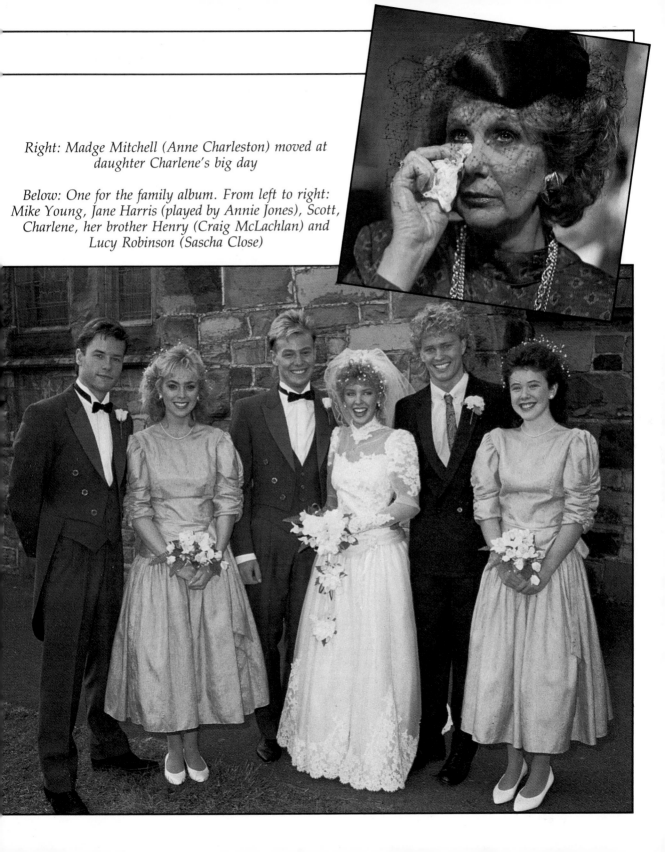

Right: Madge Mitchell (Anne Charleston) moved at daughter Charlene's big day

Below: One for the family album. From left to right: Mike Young, Jane Harris (played by Annie Jones), Scott, Charlene, her brother Henry (Craig McLachlan) and Lucy Robinson (Sascha Close)

The Mitchell family: Charlene, Madge and Henry

From the 'Will She Survive?' episode – Paul and Scott rescue Charlene from a caravan fire

Olivia Newton-John meets Kylie Minogue at the Sydney Entertainment Centre celebrating Australia's Bicentenary in the presence of the Prince and Princess of Wales

Jason and Kylie enjoy a break on the beach

The new hero of 'Neighbours' – Craig McLachlan who plays Henry Ramsay

The 'Neighbours' cast celebrate 500 episodes. From left: Sascha Close, Alan Dale, Jason Donovan, Anne Haddy and Stefan Dennis

than just the sloppily dressed girl next door. She looked like a slept-in Qantas blanket. If you're going to make a dramatic entry with a couple of hefty-handed minders the size of Ayers Rock, you should at least live up to it, not scuttle through the airport like a filthy-mooded funnel-web spider . . .'

In Kylie's defence it should be pointed out that the Sydney–London flight is a horror, the longest and most physically devastating route in the world. Strong men stagger from it as though they've gone ten rounds with Mike Tyson. As for comparing Kylie with Joan Collins, the truth is that the 'Dynasty' star only does short flights such as those from Los Angeles to London, merely commuter runs by Australian standards.

The Australian press did not take kindly to Rook's comments. The Sydney *Daily Telegraph* took up Kylie's defence in an editorial and columnist Buzz Kennedy suggested readers look in the *Concise Oxford Dictionary* for the definitions of Rook. Those who did found that they included: 'A black, hoarse-voiced crow; a cardsharp; a swindler; an extortionist; a chess piece with battle-shaped top.'

Ignoring the criticism, Kylie got down to the business of looking at the offers that had poured in. She has offers coming out of her ears. Her manager, Terry Blamey, sifts through them, tosses out the more ridiculous and discusses the remainder with Kylie.

'We look at everything on its merits,' he told *TV Week* in February 1988. 'On the recording front, we are getting requests from France and Germany. The African countries all want to know about someone who is not British who has raced to the top of the UK charts. We have had an approach from a cosmetic company for Kylie to put out her own range of make-up. There have been a number of movie offers. What Kylie would really like to do would be a contemporary movie musical – the Eighties equivalent of *Grease.* But right now we're weighing up the options. The decision is Kylie's entirely. Right now she still enjoys the show and all her friends are there.'

Blamey admits Kylie has received too much exposure. 'People start to get sick of Kylie,' he said in April 1988. 'For instance, there have been a lot of articles in recent months where journalists have just made up things because they've run out of things to say about her, and it's been damaging. It's been too much. The more exposure you get, the more negative attitudes start to flare out as well.'

But for every snide comment there are hundreds of fans ready to leap to her defence. Australia's 'Most Popular Personality' goes from strength to strength.

Jason Donovan, who won the 'Silver Logie' for Most Popular Australian Actor, congratulates Kylie

8

Jason
'*Everyone Wants to Know Him*'

Terry Donovan looked at his son and shook his head. 'Don't do it, don't become an actor,' he said. 'The whole business is too unstable.'

'But I want to do this, Dad,' said Jason Donovan. 'It's for a series called "Neighbours".'

'Okay, but don't say I didn't warn you.'

For one of the few times in his life Jason didn't take his father's advice. He felt some guilt because his father understood show business like few others in Australia, the highs, the lows, the pleasure and the pain. Terry Donovan is one of the country's leading actors, not only in films and television but on the stage, in dramatic roles and as a song and dance man – the complete professional. He has starred opposite Lee Remick in *Emma's War* and with James Coburn in *Leonski.* He was a policeman in the long-running television series, 'Division 4', has done Shakespeare and Arthur Miller and musicals ranging from *The Sound of Music* to *Chicago.* If his colleagues in the craft of acting were asked to sum up Terry Donovan in one word, they would say 'versatile'.

Jason had listened to his father's advice, but he was determined. 'He [Dad] has been in it for twenty-five years and there have been times when he's been out of work for months,' said Jason. 'But there's just something about it when you've been around it like I have that's irresistible.'

In fact, near the end of 1984, when the soap was in its planning stages, Jason was first offered a role in 'Neighbours' as Danny Ramsay, later taken by David Clencie, but Terry wanted Jason to do his final year of high school and go for his Higher School Certificate instead.

'For twelve months that boy virtually stayed at home and just put his head down and worked so hard,' Terry said proudly. 'I told him, "Don't worry if you don't get it, you are still my son, I still love you. HSC is important but it's not everything".'

Perhaps it was inevitable Jason would follow his father. He knew about cameras and lights and microphones stuck on the end of long poles when he was just a kid, because that's where he often played – in the studio while his father worked. Terry had no choice but to take his son with him on jobs. His wife had walked out leaving him a single parent.

Terry Donovan and Sue McIntosh had been known as television's glamour couple, he playing in 'Division 4' (a series in which all the cops wore hats and the crooks went bareheaded) and she a hostess on a children's series, 'Adventure Island'. In 1972 she left Terry for another man. Jason was then four. It wasn't until 1982 that Terry remarried.

The break-up deeply affected Jason. Although he resented his mother leaving, he sometimes tried to understand the reasons while at the same time keeping his distance from her. There is a trace of bitterness as he speaks. 'I have a really weird relationship with my mother. Over the years I haven't really seen her much. I only see her at Christmas and birthdays and even then not that often. When I got to fifteen I wasn't seeing much of her at all. I never sit down or get embarrassed or cry about it or feel sorry for myself because there's no reason. It's just weird because I don't know how to tackle it when people ask about my relationship with my mother. I don't understand it myself. She doesn't get along well with my father. They haven't spoken since their divorce, so it's a difficult situation. One day I'll sort it out ...'

For seven years Jason and Terry ran the home. Jason learned that if he didn't wash his dishes, no one else would, and that sometimes he had to prepare his own meals. ('I can cook up quite an omelette.') They became extremely close, each other's greatest fans.

Terry thought that Jason had 'got a big future in acting because he has got a lot going for him. He enjoys all the attention but he is a very practical boy. Jason is what he is, there are no airs and graces about him.

'I've got nothing to score off Jason. It's a fact I love him more than anyone else and he knows he can trust me more than anyone else. It doesn't matter if we have a bit of a barney. We know it will settle itself down and we'll eventually get back to square one.'

At the same time Jason feels his father is 'the only person I can trust who's been there and done it and knows a bit more about it than I do.

'He looks at the stuff I've done and he says, That's great but then again you have to think about this or that. But that's good because you come out of every scene thinking that you should have done this or that in a different way and it's terrific to have someone who knows their stuff telling you.'

As a child, Jason was in a number of TV productions, 'Golden Pennies', 'I Can Jump Puddles', 'Home', 'Marshland' and 'Skyways', appearing with a very young Kylie Minogue. Although his father insisted he take piano and drum lessons, he kept steering him away from an acting career. This was because Terry himself had left school at fifteen, working on a factory assembly line and as a labourer in a timber yard and considered an uneducated man didn't have a chance in life. 'I hated it,' Terry said of the manual jobs. 'To this day I find it an appalling thought that human beings have to live their working lives in that way.'

And so Jason became a soap opera star, perhaps not the pinnacle in an acting career but better than working on an assembly line or in a timber yard. Except the hours were longer. 'Some days I'd just like to get away from it all, sleep in, watch TV, go to the beach, be a normal person. But I couldn't sit down and relax for too long. I'd get bored. I'd have to keep working.' Some of that energy is being diverted into singing. Like Kylie, he has signed with Mushroom Records and reckons if he's half as successful in the pop world as his good friend he'll be more than pleased.

In many ways Jason has the same down-to-earth approach to life as Kylie. He tries to keep in contact with school friends, does not splash out on clothes and cars and expensive drinks, and, although he now has a house of his own, spends as much time as possible with his father in their Melbourne home. He understands that working in a soap opera does not come with a permanency clause in the contract.

'I guess I will stay with "Neighbours" for a while, I enjoy the work, it's a learning process for me more than anything, because I'm just starting out. It's experience – but it's not going to be there forever. You've got to find things over and above the show because there is going to be life after "Neighbours". When and where that will start, I don't know.

'At the moment I'm happy – content with where I'm at and what I'm learning. But if you start to think you know it all, it starts to fade away. Dad taught me that. I saw it with him – sometimes you're out of work and you have to face the fact. You're not always the flavour of the month. I've seen Dad virtually go to the dole office and say, "I need money." That's what it can be like. You can be riding the crest of a wave one minute and sinking the next. It's that type of business. It relies on people's tastes and people's tastes change. Dad's experience has given me an attitude to appreciate what I've got now and prepare for the future.'

His sudden fame meant he could not go far in public without being approached by female fans, he couldn't even go to the corner shop without being harassed. He found it both unnerving and flattering but tried to get about as well as he could, including to the beach, the summer lazing spot for most young Australians (and not a few adults), trying to be polite when fans surrounded him. 'You can't be rude to people, you have to understand how they feel. If I saw Whitney Houston walking down the street I'd go Wow! wouldn't I?'

He remains philosophical about fame and its pressures. British actor Robert Morley put it this way: 'Actors live in a cocoon. They never meet the people who don't like them.' Jason Donovan put it his way: 'You leave school and you are completely thrown out of gear and into a fast-paced workforce. You are often too tired to go out, and you tend to be more aware of going out because of the popularity of the show. Everyone wants to know you. A couple of years ago, at school, nobody could have cared less about me.'

9

Jason and Kylie
Are They or Aren't They?

Bali is popular with Australian tourists. In their tens of thousands they flock to this exquisite, mountainous 2,147-square mile of the Lesser Sunda Islands of Indonesia, mostly to lie on the beaches and drink more booze than they do at home. They show little interest in Balinese culture which centres upon religion, Hinduism fused with Buddhism, ancestor cults and belief in spirits and magic. But, still, it's a heck of a place for a holiday, which is why Jason Donovan and Kylie Minogue chose it to relax after the hectic pace of 'Neighbours'.

As they were later to discover, it was an unfortunate choice. Not only did it revive stories of the couple being an item, as gossip columnists like to say, but Kylie was photographed topless. Going topless on Balinese beaches is a tradition among young, and not so young, female Australian tourists, perhaps inspired by Balinese women who can be seen in the soft twilight bathing bare breasted in streams and rivers near their villages. Kylie no sooner had her top off than tourists, immediately recognising the couple, had their cameras clicking, some photographs later selling to newspapers for two or three thousand pounds.

The first few were sent to be developed at a photo laboratory where a worker noticed Kylie among scenes of paddy fields and temples – and copied them to sell. The Melbourne newspaper *Truth*, which published a topless photograph, quoted a tourist as saying Kylie was nearly always without the top half of her bikini. 'She looked thin and her breasts were quite small,' the tourist said. The photographs also inspired a song by Melbourne radio personality Frank N. Furter (alias actor Daniel Abineri), to the tune of Kylie's hit 'I Should Be So Lucky', called 'I Can See Your Nipples'.

What also intrigued tourists was that Kylie and Jason appeared extremely fond of each other, more than just good friends. Again to quote the anonymous tourist: 'They were nearly always alone and only seemed to have eyes for each other. Most of the time they seemed to be all over each other like any young couple together. They did a lot of kissing, cuddling and holding hands ... It was pretty plain to see they were most definitely a couple. I doubt whether you would see people who weren't going out together doing what they were doing.'

For reasons hard to fathom, the question of whether or not Jason and Kylie were having an affair intrigued devotees of 'Neighbours', both in Australia and in Britain. After all, it was not one of those grand and destructive affairs such as involved Richard Burton and Elizabeth Taylor during the making of *Cleopatra*. Not that way at all. Jason and Kylie were merely two young people who happened to like each other, but the question of were-they, weren't-they reached such astronomical proportions the British press accused the Australian press of covering up an affair to protect the couple. 'It's a romance the Australian press is keeping quiet about to ease pressure on them,' said the London *Daily Mail*.

Both deny a romance. They have denied it so many times they could record the denial and release it as a single. 'There is no steady relationship,' said Jason. 'No romance with Kylie. It's just not true. It works very well on screen because Kylie and I have known each other for so long. We have a good rapport and I think that comes through.'

Kylie had a boyfriend for about a year, but the relationship ended in early 1987, although they remain friends. She shakes her head when asked about Jason. 'We've known each other since we were twelve and worked together in "Skyways" ... it's lucky Jason and I get along as we do so much work together. But there's never been a romance – we're just good friends.' And in case people don't understand, she repeats slowly: 'Jason is not my boyfriend.'

Because they travel so much together on duties connected with promotion, they are frequently seen in each other's company, including at hotel reception desks. Being seen together at hotel reception desks means only one thing to many people. But it was only business, or as

The two 'Neighbours' stars pose frequently with each other on screen and off – here they are at Manly (Photo: News Ltd)

Kylie put it: 'I think we saw Australia fifty times over ... to be more precise, we saw the same hotel rooms fifty times over.' In Australia, still a largely chauvinistic society with quaint ideas about relationships, there was also a feeling that a male and a female could not be friends unless they were getting up to no good, as grandmother might say. So no matter how often they ran through their denials, they were not believed by many. And probably never will be.

Still, one question remains. If there is no romance, why did their management ask for a fee of around $A70,000 for the story of what, if anything, is happening between the two? A Sydney newspaper negotiated first with Jason's management for $A20,000. Then the couple joined forces and asked for $A100,000, later bringing it down to $A70,000. As it was, the newspaper thought the amount too much, even for the wonderful headlines it could have produced. If the deal had gone ahead, the newspaper was not going to pay that sum for a story on two 'good friends'.

The rumours persist. They have been that way since Scott and Charlene, the characters played by Kylie and Jason, became lovers. Their romance caught the imagination of viewers and the media, including the Sydney *Daily Mirror* which splashed it across the front page under the heading: 'Teen love scenes to shock viewers'. According to the newspaper, the scenes in which Scott asks Charlene to make love were expected 'to rock the limits of early evening viewing regulations'.

It did no such thing but, never mind, it provided much useful publicity, especially when the characters decided to live together without the blessing of church or state. Though most teenagers viewed living together as merely something that happened to some couples, the show's producers considered it a bold move for 7pm viewing. The arrangement inspired one magazine to ask: 'Should they live together? Your opinion could win you a trip to Singapore.' The magazine was possibly the first in the world to run a promotion on the subject of 'living in sin'.

What caused the concern, or at least the concern generated by the media, was that Scott and Charlene were little more than schoolkids. In fact, Scott was seventeen, rode a skateboard and went to school. Charlene, eighteen, spent most of her time under cars fixing oil leaks.

Jason and Kylie; singing – as well as acting – stars (Photo: News Ltd)

One critic suggested a more realistic storyline would have been the couple's parents 'giving their respective children a firm smack on the backside with orders to grow up.'

Kylie and Jason didn't take too much notice of the hoo-ha. They were far more practical, both saying they would rather live at home. 'As for a couple living together, I think seventeen and eighteen is a bit young,' said Kylie. 'But I certainly can't see anything morally wrong with it. I'm not old-fashioned or anything. Viewers should not see the live-in relationship as sinful because we are really trying to prove how difficult life is for teenagers when they leave the security of their parents' home.'

Jason said many of his friends were living together. 'A lot of young people do it. It's a very true picture of today's teenagers.'

Then, in the middle of 1987 Australian television screened what was hailed as television's wedding of the year. Charlene, in a gown of French chantilly lace and ivory silk organza, Scott, in charcoal grey tails, were married in an old stone church. Even some of the actors on the scene shed a small tear. But not Jason. 'I'm going to play it fairly light because I don't think the marriage will be taken seriously,' he told writer Gerri Sutton. 'They're both so young ... and I'm hanging out for the next scripts to see how the marriage goes.'

The romance and wedding did allow discussion on the question of teenage sexuality, a concern to parents ever since teenagers were known as teenagers, and before that as well. 'There should be no reason why we should not be able to tackle those sorts of issue in a drama,' Jason said. 'It's not as if we're going in there saying, Sex! Sex! – this is all we want you to watch. There is a valid moral point behind it ... Since AIDS, there's been a swing back to romance and to institutionalised relationships and I'm sure that's part of why the "Neighbours" wedding was such a hit.'

Kylie thought the marriage brought controversial subjects such as pre-marital sex and AIDS into focus. 'AIDS is changing the world,' she said. 'It's bringing back monogamy, which I think is a good thing. People are going to be much more careful and much more aware. Women know they have just as many sexual rights as men. Nowadays

Just before the Wedding of the Year – Madge Mitchell (Anne Charleston) is comforted by Ian Smith (Harold Bishop)

it's not up to the man to invite a woman to bed, she might be the one to ask him if he wants to stay with her.'

Having made the ratings shoot up for that week, the couple went away together as couples do following their nuptials. In fact Jason and Kylie did an intensive tour of Australia to promote 'Neighbours' and the wedding of Scott and Charlene. They caused riots at nearly every one of their appearances and confusion among those who had difficulty distinguishing reality from illusion. 'Oh,' a woman said loudly when she saw them in Brisbane, 'they must be on their honeymoon.'

10

Peter O'Brien and Friends

Depending on what you hear or what you read, Peter O'Brien was raised in Jervois, Murray Bridge or Tailem Bend. But the exact location is not important because they're all close by in the same area of South Australia, in dairying land near where the mighty Murray River empties into the sea after wandering 2,600 kilometres across the continent from the Great Dividing Range. In other words, he was a country boy. And proud of it.

A big name after appearing in 'Neighbours' and 'The Flying Doctors', he was invited back home as guest of honour for his home town's bicentenary celebrations and before he left drew on memories to predict what it would be like. 'On Saturday afternoon I have to toss the coin at the footie, then on Saturday night there's a cabaret in the local hall. It will be great fun, bring-your-own plate and one of the evenings where, before you know it, you can't walk because all the beer's on the floor. None of the boys will talk to the girls and at the end of the evening there'll be the obligatory two or three fights.' Never mind that it sounds like a script for a XXXX beer commercial, it happens to be the way they have fun in the bush.

Peter's a country boy. Something of a drifter, too. Leaving the cows and the rabbits he trapped for pocket money when a kid, he went to Adelaide to further his education, tossing up whether to do veterinary science at university or take an apprenticeship. 'I'd always wanted to be an actor but I thought that was completely out of my grasp. So my goal was eventually to return to farming, but Mum and Dad encouraged me to try something else first.' What he tried was a

Bachelor of Science course at Adelaide University and it was there, while studying for his degree, that his life almost ended at the age of nineteen. He became seriously ill with what the family doctor thought was glandular fever.

'I dropped down to about 50 kilograms in a matter of two or three weeks. They really thought I was gone. Then a guy who was boarding with us had an accident and when his doctor came to see him, Mum asked him to have a look at me. He put me in hospital that afternoon and operated the following day. He thought I had Hodgkin's Disease and said the only way to be certain was to remove several glands from my body and analyse them. He was very honest and said because of my condition things didn't look too good. But it turned out I had a rare disease called toxoplasmosis which is carried by pigs and cats. After the glands were removed I had to take medication for the next five years. I'm fine now, except it takes me a long time to recover from any sort of exercise.'

Back on his feet, he took up a teaching career. But he found teaching about as interesting as watching paint dry, or in his case, cows graze, and believing there was more to life, set off for the great spaces of Western Australia and the Northern Territory, hitch-hiking on the huge road trains that carry cattle along the lonely, dusty outback roads.

Eventually he arrived in Port Hedland, 1,720 kilometres north of Perth, a rough-and-tumble town from which iron ore is exported, hot as Hades, where a man is judged by his consumption of beer. A cyclone was sighted coming out of the Indian Ocean in the direction of Port Hedland, as they do with alarming frequency, causing Peter to take the advice of the experts and evacuate to Perth. There he found a message to call home.

'What's the problem, Dad?'

'No problem, son. But Grundy's want to get hold of you about that audition tape you sent them.'

'I'm on my way.'

And on his way he was, in spite of a transport strike that had him hitching again. Drawing on his experience in amateur theatre in Adelaide, he had months before sent an audition tape to the Grundy Organisation, and then forgotten about it. The tape got him a role in a short-lived series called 'Starting Out'. When the series ended after seventeen weeks, he returned to Adelaide, met up with friends but wasn't too keen on what he saw. Everyone was so organised, so settled, their lives mapped out like military targets.

So he went back to Melbourne, appearing in episodes of the established series 'Prisoner', 'Carson's Law' and 'The Henderson Kids'. In 1984 he did two auditions for 'Neighbours' and the following year moved into Ramsay Street as Shane Ramsay, a character described this way in a Ten Network press release: 'Shane Ramsay is a very together guy, despite being deprived of a normal childhood because of his father's obsession with Shane's diving training. He has an inner strength and independence and has learnt to take a stand on his father's attempts to influence him.'

His early days on television were marked by hard work and hard living. The world was at his feet and it became his personal football. It was nothing for him to arrive at work straight from a nightclub or a party, always on time, but carrying a hangover like lead weights on a racehorse or, as he admitted 'it would take two hours for my head to get there with me'. After a while he understood the two activities didn't mix and he could be out of a job, perhaps feet first.

Later his early knockabout days returned to haunt him through stories fed to the press by anonymous, obviously envious, callers. One suggested he had spent time in jail. 'I'm not saying I was a model youth,' he said. 'There was the usual, lots of partying, being a bit of a hoon, the normal things boys do. But I'm no Ronald Biggs. There have been no 28-day jail terms ... I've heard all sorts of rumours about myself – everything from the fact people have said I'm gay to I'm peddling drugs.' Unfortunately, such calls are not unusual in the small, tight world of show business in Australia and reporters spend a lot of time checking rumours. If all the rumours about some actors were true, reporters would be writing their obituaries rather than critical reviews.

Maybe a reason for the criticism was that Peter had difficulty in staying out of the headlines, whether through illnesses, cyclones or, as happened in January 1986, being interrupted while indulging in his favourite beach sport. At the time he was in Sydney promoting 'Neighbours' and took time off to go bodysurfing at Bondi Beach, the most famous and over-rated stretch of sand and surf in Australia, where swimmers can share the ocean with sewage and condoms. 'I was

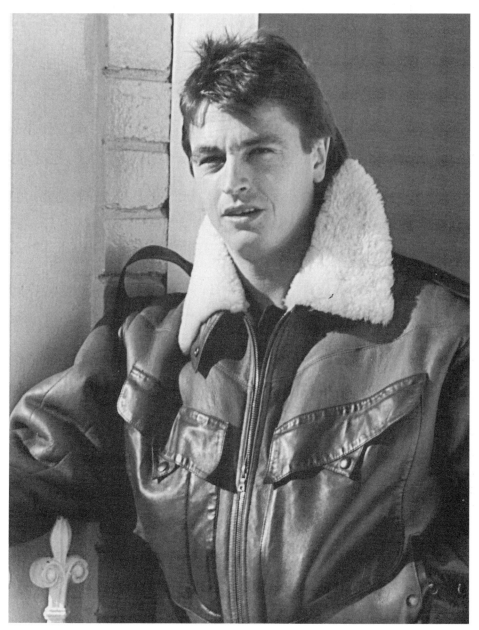

*The self-confessed world's worst flyer, Peter O'Brien, still looks
the part*

a fair way out and I heard faint screams for help and saw a man going under. I thought he was kidding but by the time I reached him he was going under and couldn't even talk. He had gone past the stage of struggling and was exhausted. I got him into the shallows and he told me in broken English he couldn't swim. I'm sure he would have died.'

Like other cast members of 'Neighbours' he was swamped by fans wherever he went, at one point confessing he'd had enough 'of my shirt being ripped off my back'. Wanting to get away from it for a while, he went to London on holiday in August 1987, planning to sleep where he could, as he had in his earlier days of wandering. This time he would doss down with friends on the floor of their flat. But he had no sooner got off the aircraft and was heading through Customs when he noticed people staring, turning, pointing, whispering like he was a terrorist with his weapons showing. Then it dawned on him. 'I knew "Neighbours" was doing well there, but I had no idea it was doing that well.'

He realised how well a few days later when walking along Oxford Street. Suddenly he noticed a mob of people following him like the cows at milking time back at Tailem Bend. 'I ducked into a shop. The owner hid me in a changing room and told the crowd I'd gone out the back way.' On another occasion while passing a shop he saw in the window a television set screening 'Neighbours'. He stopped for a look, a bit of nostalgia, a reminder of home, then glancing up he saw the entire staff of the shop staring back through the window as though he was a monkey in a cage.

And then, like many tourists, he thought 10 Downing Street would be worth an inspection. One of the duty policemen looked at him, looked again and said, 'I know you. My wife's in love with you.'

'They must be short of heart-throbs over here,' said Peter.

In some ways the adulation worried Peter because he had seen its effect on some other soap stars who expected all doors to open without an admittance fee. 'I don't like the hype and I don't like the preferential treatment. Just because I'm an actor doesn't mean I should get free admission to Joe's Bar and Grill when someone else doesn't. I know it would be easy to get carried away with it all, and without mentioning names I know plenty who have. But these people come in on a blaze of glory, expect to be given everything, and suddenly we don't see them any more. If you get carried away with it all, you end up hanging yourself.'

One of the ways Peter makes sure this doesn't happen to him is by having friends who are not in show business. To them, he's Obi, an old mate who shares their interests of surfing, sailing, horse riding and sinking the occasional beer. His family also keep him on the straight and narrow. One day his father was driving along the road and saw a huge billboard featuring Peter's face enlarged a dozen times. His father thought it the funniest thing he'd seen in a long time and rang Peter to tell him so. 'I just saw a bloody big photo of you on the side of the road,' he said. 'What are you doing up there, you drongo?'

Towards the end of 1986, Peter decided he'd had enough of 'Neighbours'. It wasn't because of an argument over money, the usual reason for actors parting company with a popular series. He simply wanted to see if there was life beyond 'Neighbours'. 'Some people stay in a show for six months and find that long enough,' he said. 'Others will remain for five years – and that's fine for them. But two years was the time I had in mind to get out.' The Grundy Organisation tried talking him out of it, fearing 'Neighbours' would suffer from his departure but he was determined to move into something new.

He thought he would be out of work for a while, that being the norm in the acting profession, but getting home one Friday night soon after he'd finally left the series in the middle of 1987 he saw a script under the door. It was for a new character called Sam Patterson in 'The Flying Doctors'. Based loosely on the Royal Flying Doctor Service, established so people living in the remotest areas of the outback could call in a medical team in an emergency, the series was one of the most popular in Australia, and in 1988 it was sold to Britain. 'My first day on set I was so nervous I could hardly remember what the character was like,' said Peter. 'I was scared about what people were going to think of me and how they would react.'

He had another problem, especially worrying for an actor playing a light aircraft pilot. 'I'm the world's worst flyer,' he confessed. 'I always expect the worst when I get in a plane and I'm always grateful to touch down.'

Having got over his fear of flying he was soon as popular with the Australian public in 'The Flying Doctors' as he had been in

'Neighbours', so much so that a wedding was arranged for his character in the fictitious town of Cooper's Crossing, the base for the flying doctors. To a great beating of publicity drums, and a little organ music, he was married to the character played by Rebecca Gibney in what, Peter insisted, was not The TV Wedding of the Year. That had already taken place in another part of Australia. 'The wedding is really low key,' he said at the time. 'There is no drama. The only person who is really excited is the priest at Cooper's Crossing. A wedding is big news for him.'

His on-screen romance with Rebecca was well liked by viewers but it caused considerable problems with his real romance. For some time Peter had been involved with Elaine Smith, who plays Daphne, the reformed stripper, in 'Neighbours'. According to British newspapers, he was having affairs with both Rebecca and Elaine. One newspaper quoted an 'insider' as saying: 'Peter is torn between two star lovers. He still loves Elaine, but he's desperately attracted to Rebecca. It isn't all over between him and Elaine, but he's spending a lot of time with Rebecca.'

When the story filtered back to Australia, Peter, Elaine and Rebecca didn't know whether to laugh or cry. Rebecca said she was sick of the whole thing. 'I can understand why people in Britain would be interested in Peter and Elaine, but why they could possibly care about me is amazing. I have never been seen in anything in Britain. I just feel sorry for Elaine. I think Elaine is a great girl and Peter and I, in spite of all this, are really good mates.' Elaine didn't think much of the story, either, admitting it hurt. 'But you have to maintain a level head. It hurt me that people could actually write that sort of thing. It put another pressure on the relationship we didn't expect.'

The affair between Peter and Elaine intrigued Australian fans of 'Neighbours' almost as much as the relationship between Jason and Kylie. It was low-key, once described by Peter as 'not as serious as everyone else sees it. There have been no slashing of wrists and promises of undying love between us. We both still lead separate private lives.' Indeed they do, Elaine living in an apartment in the fashionable Melbourne suburb of Toorak, Peter sharing a house, once a dormitory for an order of monks, with ten close friends, only two of whom are actors. 'When everyone manages to get home for dinner at

... Sometimes the stars get time off: Peter helps Annie, Kylie and Elaine improve their game

the same time we've got an instant party,' he said.

The backgrounds of Elaine and Peter were literally a world apart, he a country boy, she from Largs, Ayrshire. After graduating with an arts degree from Perth University, Elaine went to Melbourne where she appeared in a few episodes of various established TV series. Then, in 1984, wearing the short, spiky blonde hairdo that has become her trademark, she auditioned for 'Neighbours', originally for a guest spot.

'The casting director had expected me to turn up sporting long, straight hair. In fact, my different look was something he wanted for Daphne – and I became one of the five original cast members.' On the first day of recording she met Peter and 'we were attracted to each other from the start. We became friends while we were working together and started going out ...'

Daphne was described in publicity material as a 'smart intelligent girl with a strong will. She was a stripper when she came to live in Ramsay Street and now runs the local coffee shop. Daphne never talks about her family but she has obviously had a good education. She is shrewd but a warm friend.'

The idea of playing a stripper, even a reformed stripper, amused Elaine. 'She's the only stripper who's never had to take off her clothes.' The character was well received with fan magazines following and discussing her every move. Daphne was at first in love with Shane Ramsay, but then transferred her affections to Des Clarke (Paul Keane). A marriage proposal was mentioned. 'Who will win her hand?' one magazine asked breathlessly. 'Will it be Shane Ramsay or will Des Clarke be the one?'

Out there in the real land where there were more pressing problems such as balancing the family budget, avoiding street muggers and worrying about the local football team, many may not have cared less. But cheerfully joining in the game, Elaine said she didn't know whether Daphne actually needed a man in her life 'but she'd certainly got two men there. It's a triangle that's developed, but to try and give a rational explanation of it is next to impossible. Someone like Daphne would be ideal for Shane, and she has a great deal of love for him. She also loves Des, and trusts him. He's her friend.'

As it turned out, Des was the lucky fellow and in due course, with one eye on the ratings, they were married. And after a respectable period of time, thirteen actual, not soap, months, to be precise, they had a son. They called him Jamie and should have lived happily ever after, except that Elaine wanted out of the show. On the pretext of going to look after her father who was seriously ill, Daphne was written out and Elaine took a break in England where, she said, there were only two things the media wanted to know. 'One was about my relationship with Peter. The other was how much money it would take

Daphne's romantic life was the subject of much press speculation,
but Des Clarke (Paul Keane) was the lucky one (Photo: News Ltd)

for me to strip. That seemed a reasonable question to them because the character of Daphne had been a stripper.'

Daphne was asked to come back to Ramsay Street for a few more episodes to enable the loose ends to be tidied up, something which didn't often happen in some soaps in the past (where actors were suddenly fired, leaving the character wandering about in a kind of soap limbo). Elaine obliged – and Daphne was promptly in a car accident which left her in a coma. She was a long time dying, at least two days in the studio, lying in a hospital bed, bandages around her head, drips in her arm. 'It was incredibly emotional on the set,' said Elaine. 'Even I had to keep myself from crying. When the scenes were over, nobody could speak. Daphne's death was more shocking than I thought it would be but I'm glad they've completed the storyline. I don't regret the character being killed off ... I've been with "Neighbours" for two and a half years and there's a lot of other things I want to do.'

And that left the real-life situation of Peter O'Brien and Elaine Smith. The last word goes to Elaine who in the middle of 1988 said, 'Peter and I do love each other and yes, we would like to marry eventually. At the moment, our individual careers are important. We are very happy together and when the time is right, we will marry.'

With the departure of Peter O'Brien, a search began for a new 'hunk' to keep the interest of female teenagers shown by audience research to form a sizeable slice of viewers. He came in the form of Craig McLachlan, who some critics immediately dismissed as just another pretty boy. Craig heard the comments himself when on location. 'You'd hear them every now and then, they're not cruel comments, but it's blonde hair, blue eyes, dah, dah dumb. You often hear people say, "anyone can act on a soapie", but that's not the case. It's really hard work and you have to be on the ball. And you hear that expression pretty boy, but I'm not just a pretty boy. I know there's some talent there.'

Craig's role was Henry Mitchell (who later changes his name to Ramsay), son of Madge and brother of Charlene, and described by the show's producer as a charming, attractive and witty rogue. His sudden appearance was explained by the fact he had just got out of prison, a popular institution for soap producers.

Craig didn't know much about 'Neighbours' when he landed a role in the show, admitting it was not on his viewing schedule even though he was doing youth work in the country and the kids he was helping were forever discussing the activities in Ramsay Street. He'd hear names like Shane and Clive, not having a clue who they were but everyone seemed to know them like they were best friends. 'I never dreamed I'd be in the show myself.'

Born and bred in a northern New South Wales coastal town, Craig was seventeen when he first moved to Sydney, quickly landing a small role in 'The Young Doctors', a soap opera not so much over the top as somewhere out in the stratosphere. (It almost seems that at one time or another half the actors under thirty in Australia learned about the soap business from 'The Young Doctors'.) 'But at first I was naive and awestruck by the city, by the business, by everything. It was a bit too much for a country boy. I thought, If this is acting in the big city, man, you can have it. And as most teenagers do, I took the easy way out and scurried back home.' Working where he could, he got to thinking after a while there had to be more to life than unblocking toilets, carrying lumps of wood on his shoulders, picking up glasses in a bar.

He headed back to Sydney, there developing his interest in music to the point where he was in a band called The Y-Fronts, so named because of their astonishing gimmick of wearing underpants on stage, that is, underpants over trousers. Before landing the role in 1986 he was a self-confessed 'show-off' and thought it would be easy working on 'Neighbours'. 'But it was nerve-wracking. It was like going to a new school.'

However, the new school was to treat him well. And he will doubtless soon be taken to the hearts of British 'Neighbours' fans just as he has been by Australian fans.

11

Alan Dale
On Himself and Jim Robinson

In the business of soap romances – and a business they are, each kiss and cuddle carefully measured to gain the maximum ratings points – the comments of Alan Dale are worthy of note, if only because they are so succinct. Alan's character, Jim Robinson, gets to marry Bev Marshall, played by Lisa Armytage. 'I was working on the show when this new person came in,' said Alan. 'I said "how do you do?" and the next minute we are doing love scenes. Then before you know it, we're married. It's like how it must feel in India with those arranged marriages.'

Alan had been there before in the soap world. When he played Dr John Forrest in 'The Young Doctors', he was involved in highly publicised nuptials. 'It's beautifully done,' he said at the time. 'Very romantic, not sloppy at all.' His own love life has not been so smooth. His marriage broke up after ten years, and a lengthy affair with an actress and panel game hostess went the same way.

But to go back to the beginning. Alan came from the New Zealand city of Dunedin, whose citizens are so proud of their Scottish background that celebrations of Robbie Burns' birthday are major events of the year.

Moving to Auckland, he married at twenty-one, and worked at a variety of jobs including a milk run. It was while depositing bottles of milk on front door steps he found and took his chance to enter show business. 'I was driving around with the milk at 5am when I heard the breakfast announcer come on radio and announce that he was quitting. He just walked out leaving a record swishing round and round. I

*Romance for Jim Robinson comes in the form of Dr Beverly Marshall
(played by Lisa Armytage)*

finished my run, went home for a rest and shower and applied for his
job. I told them, "You need someone like me."'

Obviously they did because after allowing him to practise for two
weeks he was hired, first in the midnight to dawn graveyard shift, then
in the prime afternoon slot. In 1979, his marriage ended, he landed in
Sydney, the city of all promises.

Wasting no time, he contacted a theatrical agent the day he arrived. Within hours he was signed for a radio job and in a fortnight had a part in 'The Young Doctors'. Soon after that he met Victoria Nicolls, then hostess of the panel game 'Sale of the Century' and when he brought his sons, Mathew, then eleven, and Simon, then ten, to Australia for a holiday they helped seal the romance. 'The boys just fell in love with Victoria,' he was quoted as saying. 'They thought she was the most magic thing they'd ever seen and she fell in love with them. That was good enough for me. In any relationship I have the person has to get on with my boys because they're everything to me. Victoria really digs my kids and that's very important.'

After three and a half years he moved out of 'The Young Doctors' and went into a new series called 'Possession'. It didn't last. Out of work, he took his sons to a holiday spot on the Hawkesbury River, a waterway that wanders through bushland north of Sydney, and told them he hadn't a clue what the future held. Back home he found a message from his agent. 'Two days later I was in Melbourne working on "Neighbours".'

Originally the role was in the hands of another actor, Robin Harrison, with some scenes already shot. Contract negotiations broke down with Harrison – 'contract negotiations' cover a multitude of things in television but usually have to do with money – and Alan got the part. Scenes already filmed were reshot.

The role of Jim Robinson is vital to 'Neighbours'. In fact the role has been described as an anchor, in much the same way Leslie Grantham's part of Dirty Den is to 'EastEnders'. The character is described this way: 'Jim Robinson's wife died during the birth of Lucy and since then he has dedicated his life to ensuring that his four children have the best home life he can give them with the help of Helen Daniels. Jim is an understanding and caring father who uses reason in disciplining and educating his children. He has a great sense of fun and enjoys playing with his children. Jim is in partnership in a small engineering works.'

The part intrigued Alan because in some ways it echoed his own life. He was also a single parent, by then looking after his sons who had moved from New Zealand. 'It's like it was written for me,' he said. 'It's a great role and naturally it's one I can really relate to. You have to

Alan Dale who plays the 'vital anchor' of 'Neighbours' –
Jim Robinson

be fairly similar to a character you play, otherwise you'd go insane. But I'm not as steadfast, as straight or as patient as Jim.'

His first on-screen romance was with Zoe Davis, played by Ally Fowler. According to Ten Network publicists and the devious minds of the scriptwriters, the romance shocked Ramsay Street because Zoe was much younger and the couple had different personalities. Alan thought nothing was wrong with an older man being involved with a younger woman. 'My father lives with a girl of twenty-three and they've been together for six years,' he was quoted as saying in 1986.

However, his off-screen romance with Victoria Nicolls was not going as well. They went their separate ways, the house they shared placed on the market. 'I'm not very good at relationships,' he said soon after. 'I probably expect too much of people.'

Jim Robinson's first on-screen romance – Zoe Davis, played by
Ally Fowler

Then in a scene that could well be out of a soap script he met the 1986 Miss Australia, Tracy Pearson, nearly twenty years his junior. They ran into each other, so to speak, during practice for the 1986 Australian Grand Prix meeting in Adelaide. Alan and Tracy were not, of course, in a Formula One Ferrari, but were practising for the celebrity race, in which show business and sporting personalities spend a few laps putting dents in new saloon cars. Something of a car buff, Alan came third in the race, Tracy nowhere, but in no time they drove off together into the sunset.

Meanwhile, back on the screen, Zoe Davis became pregnant,

miscarried and departed for pastures greener than the manicured lawns of Ramsay Street. Enter Dr Beverly Marshall (Lisa Armytage). Let her explain Beverly's relationship with Jim: 'She's not even interested in him to start off with. Jim thinks he has been set up by his cousin Hilary, which makes him very much on the defensive. He's prepared for us to go out to lunch, but he treats Beverly so abominably, and she is very huffy when she realises what he thinks. So it takes a while before they start to relate to each other properly.'

'Jim had a pretty hard time of it in the show for a while there,' said Alan, 'bringing up four children. Three of his kids have now moved out of home and the last one, Lucy, is heading off to a boarding school in episodes to come. He has suddenly found himself married. His mother-in-law has moved out and his new wife's two children have entered the Robinson household. The two children in the show aren't actually Beverly's. She's bringing up her sister's children.'

As do most cast members, Alan found difficulty in coping with the public when he was out and about performing such normal and simple duties as shopping. He can be standing in a supermarket weighing up the best value in toilet paper when a fan will produce an autograph book faster than Wyatt Earp did his Colt .45. 'I was trying to load groceries into the car boot with about two minutes to make an important appointment. Someone asked me for an autograph and when I explained I was in a hurry they looked at me as if I'd crawled out from under a rock. It's really strange but when people watch and listen to you five nights a week they feel they know you as well as their own family. People will come up and say "hi!" and then realise they don't really have anything to say to you.'

He was pleasantly surprised by the success of 'Neighbours' in Britain, though this turned to unpleasant surprise when he saw various sensationalistic stories in the British tabloid press. It proved that when you're the hottest show in Britain, being approached for an autograph while loading the groceries is the least of your problems.

12

Tragedy and Illness
Myra de Groot and Anne Haddy

Jason Donovan held up his 1988 Silver Logie, awarded for Most Popular Australian Actor, and dedicated it to the courage of Myra de Groot. Eyes swivelled to where Myra had been sitting in a wheelchair at the awards but she had gone, forced by her illness to return to hospital. 'It was a very special night for Myra, but I found it very upsetting and emotional seeing her,' said Jason after the ceremony. 'It was a great thing for her to do to come here. She's so positive. She's still talking about going to London for a holiday.'

Six weeks later Jason himself was in London when he heard Myra was dead. Myra had been able to leave hospital briefly for the Logie awards. Ill for some time, she had tried not to show it. Instead she kept her sense of humour and the thoughtfulness for which she was loved around the Channel 10 studio where 'Neighbours' is shot. Craig McLachlan said she didn't 'see her illness as a great problem. She was determined to get right again.'

The way Myra saw it, her excursion to the Logies was a bonus, even in a wheelchair, because a couple of months earlier she had gone as close to death as it was possible to get without actually dying. After taking medication for a hip pain, she almost stopped breathing. It was later discovered she was allergic to the medicine. After taking the drug, Myra 'woke up choking to death. Apparently, I literally turned blue. One of the stagehands rushed me to hospital immediately and I was in the resuscitating room just like that. My Adam's apple was swollen and I had no breath. The breathing problem happened while the doctors were trying to find out exactly what was wrong with me. They said

*Jason Donovan dedicated his Silver Logie Award to the courage of
co-star Myra de Groot*

they had never heard of anyone being allergic to the medication and
there was no apparent medical reason why I should have been ... If I
hadn't gone to hospital I'd be dead.'

Doctors discovered she was suffering from a rare form of
rheumatoid arthritis usually afflicting only young children or very old
women. According to the doctor who treated her, he had seen only
two previous cases in forty years which, in spite of the pain, pleased
Myra because 'it's not every day you get such a fascinating disease'.

Of British background, Myra had travelled the world managing to
stay in an industry where the survival rate was not high. Her own

initiative got her the part of Eileen Clarke, described by the Grundy Organisation as 'Des Clarke's well-meaning but interfering mother, fifty-eight years old and divorced. She is still very hurt about her husband leaving her and is very socially conscious – particularly of her failed marriage. She is of working-class background, but has not worked since her wedding.'

Myra's character was to have been in 'Neighbours' for only a week but she thought Eileen was too valuable, too interesting, to be allowed to leave Ramsay Street. Remembering her own mother, she wrote up an expanded character and took the outline to the producers. Myra was immediately signed for a permanent position, or as permanent as they can be in a soap opera. 'I felt Eileen deserved to come back into the show,' said Myra. 'I could really see she was a very interesting lady restricted only by the binds of her generation, very similar to my mother. My mother was the strongest woman I've ever known. If she was born today she would either be the Prime Minister or they'd put her in the electric chair.'

Life's experiences helped Myra flesh out her character including episodes in which she becomes hooked on tranquilisers. Myra called on a few episodes out of her own life when she was living in Los Angeles and became hooked on sleeping pills. 'Being a chronic insomniac, I began taking them and soon I couldn't get to sleep without them. I kicked it there, but once I got back to Sydney I fell into the trap again. I went through the full withdrawal bit. It's so easy to fall victim to pills if you take one and that doesn't work and you take another. I suffered for days without sleep when I stopped taking them. I was tense, my nerves were fractured, I scratched and had the most amazing sugar binges – the whole bit.' But Myra did not die from her previously diagnosed condition. It was cancer that killed her in the end.

Another with more than her fair share of health problems was Anne Haddy, a veteran actress who had appeared in many stage productions – including *Hostile Witness* with Ray Milland – in movies, television dramas and soaps. In 'Neighbours' she plays Jim Robinson's mother-in-law, Helen Daniels, decribed thus: 'When her daughter died, Helen's heart went out to Jim and his four children and she took over the running of the house. Helen has been widowed for fifteen years. She is an avid reader with a strong interest in world affairs and politics,

*Anne Haddy, survivor of many serious illnesses, with Kylie Flinker
(the first Lucy Robinson)* (Photo: News Ltd)

and is an accomplished amateur artist. However, the core of her life is
the well-being and happiness of the Robinson family.'

When Anne once said soap characters had 'to have struggles, tears,
conflicts,' she could well have been talking about herself. Back in 1971
Anne was appearing in a Sydney stage production when during
rehearsals she fell and broke her wrist. Fortunately help was at hand
because the play was *National Health* by Peter Nichols, set in the public

ward of a London hospital and at rehearsals were a number of nurses to instruct the cast in techniques.

Then in 1979 she collapsed from a heart attack in the kitchen of her Sydney home. Years later she could laugh and say her only regret was that the ambulance drove slowly to the hospital instead of belting along with siren blaring. 'I was absolutely furious. I had waited all my life to travel in an ambulance and when I did they didn't use the siren at all.' After undergoing a bypass operation, she was no sooner on her feet than she fell and broke a hip.

Then came cancer. Feeling a slight discomfort in her side, she went for tests and found she had cancer in the wall of her stomach. Because it was detected early, doctors were able to remove the growth safely.

In 1983 she was in hospital again, this time to unclog one of her four heart bypasses. Six weeks later she was back working in the soap 'Sons and Daughters'. 'I asked the producer to ease me in. The first day was fine, very slow. But that was the end of my holiday. The second day back on set I was in almost every scene. At the end of the day I felt tired – and wonderful.'

Now Anne treats every day as a bonus. 'It sounds corny, but we are thankful for every single day. After my first bypass operation I thought my whole world was just unfixed. It was only because of a wonderful advancement of science that I survived it. I should be dead ... I'm grateful to be alive. It sounds a bit trifling, but to wake up every morning with the birds is a joy.'

After the illnesses that would have sent many to bed for the remainder of their lives, Anne refused to give up work on the grounds she would suffer from terminal boredom. She joined 'Neighbours' as one of the original cast, was settling in nicely, having moved from Sydney to Melbourne with her husband, actor James Condon, when she was told the soap was to be cancelled.

'My heart fell to the floor. Jim and I had moved all our furniture from Sydney to Melbourne and the thought of packing up again was too much.' She was saved by an angel in the form of the Ten Network and to make life more pleasant her husband also joined 'Neighbours'. 'So here I am, working like a dog and loving every minute of it. Everybody is very kind. People are wonderful to me in the studio. They don't treat me like an old crock. Sometimes, though, I feel like one.'

13

The Ramsay Street Regulars

In and out of the swinging doors of 'Neighbours' go the actors, some staying briefly, others for years, some leaving because they want a career change, others through no choice of their own. Francis Bell left 'Neighbours' because of a sore back that came from an injury, which in true soap style, occurred only a week before he married his longtime fiancée in April 1986. 'I always thought one suffered a bad back after one's wedding,' he said cheerfully between groans on the day of his nuptials. 'I've had a history of slipped discs and other back ailments. I suppose I should have had something done about it.'

Francis should have been set for a long run. He was there at the beginning as Max Ramsay, described as 'a self-employed plumber. Beneath his rough, tough façade, he is not sure of himself. Max survives by trying to dominate situations. He approves of those who comply and feels those who resist are stupid. He would nearly always defend, justify or avoid the issue of his having done anything wrong, stupid or thoughtless. Behind all this, Max is a man with basically good intentions in life. Ramsay Street was named after Max's grandfather. Consequently, Max has a personal pride in "his" street – and who lives there.'

Francis based his character on a person who helped bring him up in New Zealand, where he spent his childhood before moving to Australia. 'Max is based on a man whom I loved, but who gave me a very hard time. Playing Max is going back to my roots in a way. I was brought up in a working-class extended family and it was only through scholarships and a lot of hard work that I broke the cycle.'

Some British critics have suggested that as a plumber Max would not be able to afford the comfortable lifestyle of Ramsay Street. What surprised Australians was why a plumber chose to live in such a modest area when he could make his home among the silvertails. Plumbers in Australia earn the sort of money to which doctors and lawyers aspire.

Before going into 'Neighbours', Francis's acting had a Shakespearean ring to it, the result of studying acting and mime in England. He enjoyed the down-to-earth activities of 'Neighbours' because 'it's the comedy and drama of real life. But working in it requires so much energy. You can't live a normal life. You're up at five most mornings, then by the time you finish taping and get home and get started learning the next day's lines, it's usually after midnight.'

Suddenly, in the middle of 1986, Max was written out of the show. Rumours quickly spread in a business that feeds on rumours and rumours of rumours. It was said in show business circles that Francis did an Oliver Twist and asked the Grundy Organisation for more, in this case money, and that Grundy's said no. This was partly true. Francis and Grundy's could not agree on a new contract. But as Francis explained it also had to do with his back pains. 'I was considering resigning before my back problems flared up. Negotiations had been under way between my agent and Grundy's for some time and I had decided I didn't want to do the show any more.' Francis found it more difficult each day to get into the character of Max. Some actors can slip into their characters like one would an old overcoat but Francis found he had to psych himself up each day. It was no longer a pleasure but damn hard work.

'I can't just sort of drop into Max. I can do his voice, but to preserve the integrity of the character while churning out two and a half hours of television a week was always hard,' he said. 'The back injury hadn't been treated properly and I hadn't had decent sleep for over a year. I have no regrets about having done "Neighbours". It's a good show and I learned what was involved in doing a soap opera and that's been invaluable. I wanted to do a major role in a long-running series, I'd knocked them back for years. "Neighbours" was a good experience and there's some bloody nice people in the cast of that show.'

Another who came and went, and had no regrets, was Geoff Paine. A spiky-haired young man, he was discovered in the classical manner by the Grundy Organisation, while performing in a college production at the Victoria Arts Centre. 'The producer and a couple of people from the casting agents saw the play and called me for a screen test at Grundy's,' he said. A month later he had the part of Clive Gibbons, which meant he had to spend not a little time in a gorilla suit. Clive ran a Gorillagram agency from the house he rented next door from the Ramsay family, that is, he delivered birthday greetings and such while dressed in his unlikely costume. Max was not amused. 'The first time Max meets Clive he's wearing a gorilla costume, loading two girls dressed as chooks [chickens] into a little beat-up Mini on the way to a job,' Geoff explained. 'Max is pretty perplexed by this guy with these chickens and thinks the place has been turned into a zoo.'

After more than a year, Geoff declined to renew his contract on the grounds he was in danger of being typecast, not only as Clive but as a gorilla. 'I don't regret leaving "Neighbours" at all,' he said. 'I think it's terrific the way the show's taken off, but I'm very pleased with the direction I've taken.'

Vikki Blanche, travelling along nicely in her role of Julie Robinson, left for much the same reason as Geoff Paine. She wanted more than 'Neighbours' could offer. 'When the series started, I knew I didn't want to stay for the full twelve months. I learnt a lot from "Neighbours" but it also retards your development staying in the same role for so long. I want to make sure I experience as much as possible so I know what I want.'

Her character was seen as a nosey gossip, nasty, something of a bitch. But she wasn't so irritating as Mrs Mangel, played by Vivean Gray. Every soap opera has a sticky-beak character like Mrs Mangel, the classic example being Ena Sharples of 'Coronation Street'. Mrs Mangel's main task is to stir up the street, interfere, get everyone talking. This allows the scriptwriters ample opportunities to create scenes out of the thin air of gossip.

Anne Charleston, who admits she was 'stage struck from birth', came into 'Neighbours' as Max Ramsay's elder sister, Madge Mitchell. According to the storyline, 'Max has always found his sister to be formidable, and he never wins with her around. Madge has no time for failure, frivolity, waste, laziness or any other obstacles that could get in her way. She is very much a social climber. She fails to find most things funny, especially jokes made at her expense, which Max thrives on. Madge is rather keen on Jim Robinson.'

The course of human history changes daily in soaps, and Madge has developed into a more appealing character. Anne herself is a single mother, with a son, Nicholas, eighteen, and a fourteen-year-old niece, Emma, whom she took into the family when Emma's mother died of cancer. Sometimes the similarities of her life and that in Ramsay Street were so remarkable Anne felt she was taking her work home. 'At the time, in the show, when Madge was having problems of whether or not Charlene should leave school, I was having the same sort of arguments at home. I wanted Nick to stay on at school but he really wasn't interested. I can't complain, though. Within two months he had a job and he's already saving.'

Putting into practice the theory you don't go to the greengrocers to buy nails, Grundy Organisation representatives can often be found at theatre workshops, the supermarket, if that is not too vulgar a description, of new talent. Something fresh. And not too expensive. At a Saturday morning workshop of the National Drama Theatre in Melbourne they found Charlene Fenn, then seventeen. She was signed for the part of Helen Daniels' niece, Nikki Dennison, who moved quietly into Ramsay Street. 'Nikki's widowed mother works in a bar to send her to a good boarding school,' said Charlene. 'But Nikki doesn't really appreciate this because she feels her mum has forced her into a position where she has to lie to be accepted by other girls.'

Charlene believed the two sides of Nikki made her a more interesting character. One a genuine and charming person without a need to impress, the other with nasty elements of bitchiness, snobbishness and social climbing. Unfortunately for Charlene, her character went out of the swinging doors in less than a year, leaving her to philosophise: 'I never thought I was going to be employed in this for the rest of my life.'

Annie Jones had a longer life as Jane Harris, the girl who seems to be fancied by most of the lads in Ramsay Street. Annie explained the love tangles of her character, and to avoid confusion one must read carefully because love life wasn't meant to be easy in 'Neighbours'.

'Plain Jane' Harris (Annie Jones) who became the pin-up of Ramsay Street, and dated Mike Young (Guy Pearce) (Photo: News Ltd)

'Jane has always fancied Scott, even from early school days, but because of her friendship with Charlene she was satisfied to go out with Mike instead. Henry has always admired Jane. Scott and Jane think that Henry has seen them together, Charlene cracks a mental and, because of the guilt, Scott and Jane spill the beans.'

Annie was originally signed for six weeks in 1986 but the producers thought her character worthy of a longer life and she became one of the regulars. 'When I first started I was pretty plain but now I'm glam Jane,' said Annie. Her popularity was such that it rubbed off on her parents, who migrated to Australia from Hungary nearly forty years ago and now live in the quiet Brisbane suburb of Bray Park. Proud of their daughter, they are nevertheless bemused by all the attention. 'People have asked me for my autograph,' said Annie's mother, astonished at their behaviour. 'I try to tell them I am just her mother but they insist I write my name.'

Ally Fowler came into 'Neighbours' after a stint in 'Sons and Daughters'. For a while she kept body and soul together by waitressing but was then approached by the Grundy Organisation for the part of Zoe Davis, described as 'fickle and unpredictable to an incredible degree. She has a sharp wit and a blunt tongue, although not heartlessly so. Romance is the only game she really likes to play and this she pursues most of all, but not always wisely. She longs to be "truly in love" but it keeps eluding her.'

Ally's concern was that soaps can typecast an actress, the reason she left 'Sons and Daughters'. 'I don't want to get tied to a show again for as long as I was with "Sons and Daughters",' she said at the time. 'I really miss acting, some of the people in the show and, sometimes, the money, but I don't miss the premières and parties. I only ever went to them if I had to. I don't like the glitter and pretentious side of show business. I'm not into promoting myself.'

She was in 'Neighbours' for more than a year, leaving with the comment: 'I worked with a great bunch of people on "Neighbours" and I really miss them but I prefer not to do so many long runs in a soap for a while.'

In this age of sexual equality, 'Neighbours' played its part by providing several young males over whom female viewers can swoon or fantasise, or both. One was Guy Pearce, who walked straight out of school into his role of Mike Young, although that is putting it much too simply. Raised in Geelong, an industrial town across Port Phillip Bay from Melbourne, he was involved in amateur theatre at school and had roles in several musical comedies. Pursuing his acting ambitions, he bombarded the Grundy Organisation with audition tapes, including a tertiary education promotional tape shown in Victorian schools in which he played a university student. The tape clinched his contract.

According to the official biography, Guy's character, Mike, was 'a

Ex star of a band called The Y-Fronts ... Craig McLachlan

thoroughly nice young man. Scott Robinson recommends him for the job at the coffee shop which he does outside school hours. He is ambitious and hardworking, and often studies in the coffee shop. One of the motivations behind taking the job is to earn money to get himself and his mother away from his father, who bashes both Mike and his mother.'

One of the reasons for the female interest in Guy was his physique, developed over years of pumping iron and avoiding junk food. At sixteen he won the Mr Teenage Victoria bodybuilding title and has built a gymnasium in the garage of his home to work out. He likes swimming but found it could sometimes be difficult because of the popularity of 'Neighbours'. 'I finish my laps and there standing at the end of the pool are about twenty girls. I tend to go places by myself and that's when the girls strike. But I think everyone has to admit it gives you a buzz to be recognised.'

His early life wasn't easy. In 1976, when Guy was eight, his father, Stuart Pearce, chief test pilot for the Australian-built Nomad aircraft, took off from a Victorian airfield. Minutes later the aircraft crashed into a muddy paddock beside the runway. Stuart Pearce was killed. Guy, the only male in the family, sometimes speculates as to how his father would view his acting career. 'I often wonder how he would react ... He used to be one of the boys and sort of frowned upon actors.'

Music is Guy's main interest, shared by several others in the cast of 'Neighbours', including Craig McLachlan, Paul Keane, David Clencie, Jason Donovan and, of course, Kylie Minogue. Guy studied music for his Higher School Certificate and plays saxophone, keyboard and guitar. 'When I leave "Neighbours" I would like to start my own group,' he said. 'But I won't knock back any acting right now.'

When Stefan Dennis auditioned for 'Neighbours', he was interested in the role of Shane Ramsay. It went to Peter O'Brien. 'Then they asked me to come back and read for the part of Des Clarke. I went away on holiday, came back and found out I was to be Paul Robinson.' The character was described as one who was 'once considered the ponderous "quiet achiever" of the Robinson family, and has become bitter and self-centred. The dramatic change is the result of his traumatic relationship with his wife Terri. Terri is in jail on a murder charge. This has left Paul emotionally scarred.'

Raised on the Gold Coast, the Australian equivalent of Miami, Stefan heeded the wise words of his father who said, 'Son, there are two trades in which you'd never be out of work – food and undertaking.' Not liking the idea of dealing with the dead, he trained as a chef, working in restaurants on the Gold Coast and on Daydream Island on the Barrier Reef. While cooking in a Gold Coast restaurant he met his wife, Roz, a model and panel game hostess. 'In the same complex as the restaurant was a nightclub that we all haunted after work,' he said. 'This may sound like a fairytale but one night I looked up and walking into the club was this absolutely stunning girl. That was it for me.'

Always at the back of his mind was the notion acting would be a desirable occupation. In 1978 he went to Melbourne where he worked in several soaps and series. Between acting jobs, or while 'resting' as actors like to describe the non-working periods of their irregular lives, he was pleased he had heeded his father's advice. Several times he was forced back to the pots and pans to support himself.

He is outspoken on social issues, especially nuclear war. The very fact that world leaders can even visualise nuclear war appals him. 'War, and especially nuclear war, is irrational and it seems even more irrational that anyone with the level of power of Reagan or Gorbachev is going to wipe everything, including themselves, out. I'm an anti-violent person. Basically I like to think of myself as a pacifist. It's shocking to think that people speak about war as just another thing that happens.' Because he struggled to establish his acting career, as well as training to be a chef, he believes that kids are not helping themselves enough when it comes to employment. 'I think there's a lot of young people who are taking the easy way out. We all get out of school and can't get a job. It's easy to blame it on the unemployment situation but why not generate employment, either for yourself or others? If you're ambitious enough you'll get there.'

David Clencie was twenty when he got the role of sixteen-year-old Danny Ramsay. 'He's an interesting character to play, a bit different from all the others,' said David. 'There are so many different sides to him. He's brash and wild on the outside, but underneath quite troubled and confused.'

David was a little wild and brash himself. In a revealing interview with leading Australian show business writer Kevin Sadlier, he told how the death of a close friend from a heroin overdose had a profound effect on his life. 'I think I could have been heading in the same direction,' he said. 'It affected me deeply but what is more important, it made me stop and think. I learnt a lot from his death. I learnt that drugs add up to a waste of young souls. He had to die in order that so many of us who were left could live. There were probably forty or fifty of us who knew him and it was a warning to us all. The tragedy is that probably only about thirty of us heeded that warning. The rest haven't learnt enough to leave drugs alone.' Formerly with a rock band, The Scream, he wrote a song about his friend's death, called 'Beautiful Waste'.

While working on 'Neighbours', he formed a relationship with Vikki Blanche (Julie Robinson) and supporting the theory two can live as cheaply as one, they moved in together for six months. After more than a year, David's character was written out of the soap, the parting, according to David, by mutual agreement. 'I was offered three different contracts with the show but after discussion it was decided I would take a break', he was quoted as saying. 'I have made errors and I have had an unprofessional attitude in the past. There were times when I did let the actors, the company down. I refused to get my hair cut and wear the wardrobe they provided for Danny. But I learnt from that . . .'

Perhaps the most private person in 'Neighbours' is Paul Keane, who plays Des Clarke, 'the 28-year-old son of Eileen Clarke. He came from Perth to live at 28 Ramsay Street and is well acquainted with the Robinson family – especially Paul, with whom he had become good friends. Des has had four serious relationships with women and all of them have ended in disappointment for him. Twice his mother ruined his relationships for him in Perth. Although Daphne Lawrence has declared her love for him, he is nervous about making a commitment.'

A graduate of the National Institute of Dramatic Art, Paul had played in *Romeo and Juliet* and *The Cherry Orchard*. Although actors have to work where they can, Paul's decision to go into 'Neighbours' seemed strange. He doesn't even like neighbours, the ones out there in the real world, that is, not those in Ramsay Street. 'It's not personal,' he said. 'It's just that I'm a very private kind of person and I don't appreciate the people from next door barging in and expecting cups of tea.'

This wouldn't do for Ramsay Street where the neighbours are likely

Ex neighbours – Vikki Blanche and David Clencie (Photo: News Ltd)

to barge in any time of the day or night. And not merely for a cup of tea. Their missions to the houses next door usually involve a crisis of some sort, more often than not to do with their love lives. They don't want a cup of tea but a shoulder to cry on, a sympathetic ear to listen, an audience for their complaints. This is the very essence of 'Neighbours'.

How long will they continue to act in this manner? A soap opera has a life of its own, the length of which depends on the ingenuity of the writers and the fickleness of the public. Near the end of 1987, Grundy Organisation chief Ian Holmes was asked about the future of 'Neighbours'. He thought then it had at least one good year at the top of the ratings in Australia before it began to fade. But that was before 'Neighbours' was moved to the evening spot in Britain and began drawing an audience no one could have imagined. It is likely the Ramsays, the Robinsons, the Clarkes, their relatives and friends and the occasional blow-in will live much longer.